FUTURE VISIONS

To my parents,
whose lifelong devotion
to education inspired this project

FUTURE VISIONS

The Unpublished Papers of
Abraham Maslow

Edited by
Edward Hoffman

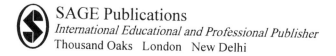

SAGE Publications
International Educational and Professional Publisher
Thousand Oaks   London   New Delhi

For information address:

SAGE Publications, Inc.
2455 Teller Road
Thousand Oaks, California 91320
E-mail: order@sagepub.com

SAGE Publications Ltd.
6 Bonhill Street
London EC2A 4PU
United Kingdom

SAGE Publications India Pvt. Ltd.
M-32 Market
Greater Kailash I
New Delhi 110 048 India

Printed in the United States of America

Library of Congress Cataloging-in-Publication Data

Maslow, Abraham H. (Abraham Harold)
    Future visions: The unpublished papers of Abraham Maslow /
editor, Edward Hoffman.
        p.   cm.
    Includes bibliographical references and index.
    ISBN 0-7619-0050-0 (cloth). — ISBN 0-7619-0051-9 (pbk.)
    I. Hoffman, Edward [DATE].   II. Title.
BF109.M33A25   1996
150.19′8—dc20   95-50154

This book is printed on acid-free paper.

96 97 98 99   10 9 8 7 6 5 4 3 2 1

Project Editor: Christina Hill
Cover Designer: Candice Harman

Related Books
by Edward Hoffman

The Drive for Self:
Alfred Adler and the Founding of Individual Psychology

The Right to Be Human:
A Biography of Abraham Maslow

The Way of Splendor:
Jewish Mysticism and Modern Psychology

Visions of Innocence:
Spiritual and Inspirational Experiences of Childhood

Wilhelm Reich:
The Man Who Dreamed of Tomorrow

Contents

PART I
Personality, Growth, and Therapy

PART II
Re-Visioning Psychology

PART III
Management, Organizations, and Social Change

Foreword

I think it significant that in more than a quarter of a century since Maslow's death, there has been no sign of a decline in his reputation, whereas Freud's and Jung's are heavily bullet scarred. This, I believe, is because there is a sense in which Maslow has *still* not come into his own. His significance lies in the future and will become apparent in the 21st century.

In my book on Maslow, *New Pathways in Psychology* (1982), I describe a letter I received from him in 1959 explaining that he had read a book of mine called *The Stature of Man* and that my idea that modern literature was debilitated by what I called "the fallacy of insignificance" resembled an idea of his own that he called "the Jonah Complex." He has once asked his class, "Which of you believe that you will achieve greatness?" When they stared at him blankly, he asked, "If not you, *who* then?"

He enclosed some of his papers, and I was immediately impressed by the one on the peak experience. It was obvious to me that he had taken an enormous step beyond Freud, Jung, and Adler—although Adler's concept that we possess a "will to health" came close to it. I replied, and we began to correspond. In due course (in 1966, I think) we met when he invited me up to Brandeis, when, like everyone else, I was captivated by his gentle charm. Unfortunately, we never met again, for I was back in England for most of the remainder of the 1960s. But we remained in touch by mail.

I cannot now recall which of us proposed a book about him—or whether the suggestion came from a publisher—but I remember that we both thought it an excellent idea. Abe died while I was still working on it, but by then he had sent me half a dozen tapes full of autobiographical reminiscences and a huge box of his papers, many unpublished. As I finished the book, I felt that some benign fate had intervened in 1969 to suggest the idea while Abe was still alive to collaborate. It is still just about my favorite among my nonfiction books.

In retrospect, what amazes me was that he succeeded in becoming an establishment figure in the course of his lifetime. He told me on a number of occasions that it amazed him, too. Freud, Jung, Adler, and Reich achieved their celebrity as practicing physicians who claimed to understand what caused psychological problems. They had, so to speak, a ready market for their wares. Abe was a teacher all his life, and, as far as I know, never had any patients. His work in academic psychology—S–R Theory and so on— was fairly early in his career. So with his belief that human nature has "higher ceilings" and that Freud "sold human nature short," he might well have been dismissed as a vague idealist who had no right to call himself a psychologist. Fortunately, this never happened—at least, as a consensus—and while I was teaching at the University of Washington, in Seattle, in 1967–1968, I had the pleasure of seeing a pile of Abe's "Toward a Psychology of Being" standing beside the cash register in the bookstore, selling as fast as a popular novel.

If I now had to explain what I believe to be his essential contribution, I would say that it lay in advancing the most important picture of the human psyche since Freud. We are all agreed—even those who detest Freud as much as I always have—that Freud brought about a revolution in psychology by grasping the role of the unconscious mind. It was as important as adding some new continent to the map of the world. It is true that dozens of others had recognized the unconscious before Freud, from Leibniz to F. W. H. Myers and William James, but Freud somehow turned it into a solid fact, like Antarctica.

The problem, as Aldous Huxley pointed out, was that Freud's picture of the human psyche was a kind of "bungalow with cellar," the cellar being full of rats and decaying refuse. Myers had suggested that man also possesses an "attic"—what might be called the superconscious mind—but because his primary interest was in psychical research, the idea never achieved any currency.

Maslow was the first to state clearly that human beings have psychological needs that Freud would have dismissed as "sublimations": the need for creativity, for long-term purpose, for values, for goodness. In doing so, Maslow created a completely new map of human nature. According to Freud, a human's most basic need is sex, and all neurosis—not just *some* of it—is

due to sexual problems. Reich took a step in the right direction by recognizing that these sexual needs are somehow connected to our highest aspirations
and that through the sexual impulse, we have an almost mystical glimpse of
what we might become. Jung went further still in stating that "man has a
religious function," an obscure need for transcendence.

But when Maslow stated emphatically that all healthy people have "peak
experiences," and that these are *not* "mystical" experiences but a normal
part of everyday life, he was offering a new vision of human nature. In stating that humans have a "hierarchy of needs," ranging from food and security
and sex and self-esteem to self-actualization, he was recognizing that the
root of neurosis was the fundamental human need to achieve some kind of
creativity.

I hasten to add—what Abe knew as well as I do—that creativity need not
involve writing symphonies or poems. The anthropologist Edward T. Hall
noted in his book *The Dance of Life* that "for the Quiche, living a life is
somewhat analogous to composing music, painting, or writing a poem. Each
day properly approached can be either a work of art or a disaster." This is
something that Maslow had also learned from his time among the Blackfoot
Native Americans.

In other words, self-actualization lies in a certain attitude of mind. It can
be experienced by a Michelangelo or by a retired carpenter putting ships in
bottles or even a housewife tidying her new home. But it involved a *flow* of
creative energy, which in turn brings not only satisfaction but mental (and
probably physical) health.

In Maslow's view, people have not only a fundamental "will to health,"
but also—to put it as provocatively as possible—a will to do good to others.
I am not speaking of simple altruism, for the music of Arnold Schoenberg
and the logical demonstrations of Kurt Godel also qualify. Shaw, speaking
of philosophy, said, "Our minds are nothing but this knowledge of ourselves,
and he who adds a jot to such knowledge creates new mind as surely as any
woman creates new men." One of Shaw's worst plays, *The Shewing Up of
Blanco Posnet,* is on the same theme: a criminal who gives up his old ways
because he recognizes that he has a deep inner drive to do good rather than
evil, to be unselfish rather than selfish.

It seems to me that this was Maslow's greatest contribution: to recognize
that *all* human beings possess a "higher nature" and that fulfillment depends
on acknowledging the existence of this higher nature. In making this recognition the basis of his psychology, Maslow was turning is back on more than

two centuries of the opposite assumption. After Newton and Descartes, philosophy set out to liberate itself from the old religious notions about God and the Devil. The result was the philosophy of human nature that claimed to be realistic because it dismissed goodness, unselfishness, and altruism as sentimental delusions. Charles Lamb remarked that nothing is more delightful than to do good by stealth and have it found out by accident. The sentiment behind this witticism—the implication that we cannot help acting selfishly even when we are "doing good"—was given scientific justification by Darwin's doctrine of the survival of the fittest.

So Freud's demonstration that all human impulses must be reduced to the lowest common denominator was an expression of an opinion that was held by most intelligent people in the late 19th century. Jung describes how he protested Freud's view that all art and "spirituality" is merely an expression of repressed sexuality, pointing out that it would "lead to an annihilating judgment upon culture," and how Freud replied, "Yes, and that is just a curse of fate against which we are powerless to contend."

At this point, I must add that I have always found it incomprehensible that Maslow always expressed respect and admiration for Freud and even described himself as a "Freudian." Was it because he was afraid that open rejection of Freud would make his position as a psychologist untenable and he decided that a certain protective coloration was necessary? He certainly disagreed with Freud even more basically than Jung or Adler did, and his own belief in "higher ceilings of human nature" was simply an open contradiction of everything Freud stood for. Or perhaps it was a kind of artistic appreciation of the sheer power and coherence of Freud's life and work, which certainly makes a compulsively readable story. Of course, we have to remember that when Maslow was a young psychologist, Freud had been placed on a scientific pedestal alongside Darwin, Rutherford, Einstein, and Planck and remained the dominating force in American psychology throughout the 1940s and 1950s.

Whatever the reason, I suspect that if Maslow were still alive today—and he would be only 87—he might well take a less charitable view of Freud.

It certainly seems to me a tragedy that Maslow died at the age of 62, just as his work was beginning to achieve widespread appreciation. This present volume shows that hi restless mind was always attacking new problems. One of his last essays, on "Biological Injustice and Free Will," is almost theological in its implications, particularly this sentence: "The individual does not have to be victorious to be accepted by the gods." Maslow is here asking whether people who are born with some awful defect are not a living disproof of his optimistic view of human nature. His answer—that whatever happens, we possess free will—echoes Sartre's assertion that even a man dying of cancer can decide when he gives in to the pain. Again and again, as I read Maslow, I believe that he belongs to the great Jewish tradition of the "wise man," the tradition to which Spinoza and Moses Mendelssohn belonged. (And both, of course, were "biologically disadvantaged.")

I suspect that if Maslow had succeeded in living out the normal human life span, he would have devoted an increasing amount of time to pulling together his many insights into a coherent whole. I am not, of course, suggesting that his work is incoherent. But anyone who reads this volume— surely as important as anything he published in his lifetime—will see that it is full of marvelous ideas that seem to demand exploring in a wider context. He speaks, for example, of counseling a young man who said, "If that car had hit me, all my troubles would not be over," and pointing out "all the lovely problems," all the "pleasant tortures of life" the young man would have missed. What seems to be demanded here is some wider recognition that the most basic of our human problems is a kind of tunnel vision that traps us in the present moment, like a person lost in some huge city where high buildings continually block the view; what we need here is clearly the equivalent of a city map, with a list of streets. Anyone who experienced as many flashes of insight as Maslow would have been the ideal person to settle down to drawing such a map.

I continue to feel that there was a sense in which Maslow had solved the basic problem to which all his work was addressed and that he still failed to recognize it. For example, the essay on "The Psychology of Happiness" begins by mentioning the need for a wider definition of happiness than the notion of having pleasure without pain. He goes on to speak of the "grumbles threshold" and mentions my own concept of the "St. Neot's margin," or indifference threshold. I had noted that there seems to be an area of consciousness that is indifferent to pleasant stimuli but that *can* be jarred into perception of values by some threat or prospect of disaster. Maslow asks perceptively whether it is possible to be happy and not know you are happy— and, of course, the answer is that we do it all the time. But how could we learn to *perceive* this when we are bogged down in the present moment with its trivial problems?

It has always seemed to me that the human problem can be simply expressed. We are at our best when faced with interesting or exciting challenges. Everyone longs for a more creative, a more productive way of life. Yet when external problems vanish, we tend to sink into a kind of sloth.

So we seek out "purposes," which usually means interesting complications, to keep us satisfied. But it is all too easy to find a purpose that keeps you interested but basically wastes your life—let us say, for example, giving endless dinner parties and inviting other people to yours until you never spend an evening alone.

So human beings find themselves faced with a not particularly helpful choice: being pleasantly "involved" but condemned to waste whole slabs of valuable time or being "uninvolved" but paralyzed by boredom and lack of purpose.

Yet there is a third possibility. Human beings differ from the animals in that they do not lead a wholly physical existence. They have learned to use their minds and imaginations and can spend hours alone, yet totally fascinated by ideas or even fantasies. (While Tolstoy was writing *War and Peace,* he obviously spent weeks or months in a world inside his own head.)

It seems to me that humanity has reached a point in its evolution where the most urgent necessity is to learn the truck of plunging into a state of "fascination" (i.e., mental involvement) while remaining alone and personally uninvolved. H. G. Wells remarked, "The fish is a creature of the water; the bird is a creature of the air; man is a creature of the mind." But until we learn that trick of plunging into these "inner" states at will, this will remains untrue; we will remain creatures who are enslaved to the external world.

Now is seems to me that Maslow came closer to solving this problem than anyone I can think of; he did this by recognizing the importance of the peak experience.

My favorite Maslow anecdote is of the young mother who was watching her husband and children eating breakfast when a beam of sunlight came in through the window, and she thought, "My God, aren't I *lucky!*" and went into the peak experience. (I have a vague feeling that Maslow didn't mention the beam of sunlight in the published version. If so, I see why not. A trigger *can* be useful, but it isn't necessary. We can acquire the knack of triggering ourselves.)

The point is that she was lucky *before* the beam of sunlight came in, but she didn't *realize* it. This, in turn, makes us aware that we all have a thousand reasons for feeling lucky; yet we can feel bored or even depressed, merely because we fail to *focus* on them.

But how can we acquire the knack? Again, Maslow found the answer. He describes how he got his students to describe peak experiences they'd had in the past and then forgotten about. In other words, they took the experiences for granted, as something pleasant but not all that important. Then as they began to describe peak experiences and listen to those of others, an interesting thing happened: They began having peak experiences all the time. Merely focusing on peak experiences, and regarding them as a normal and necessary part of life, did the trick.

I do not know whether Maslow recognized the immense significance of what he had stumbled on. But it seems to me that whether he did or not, he had stumbled on the secret of the next step in human evolution.

And here, although space is running out, I must mention briefly another discovery that strikes me as being of comparable significance. The Chicago psychologist Eugene Gendlin has developed a technique that he calls "focusing." He persuades patients to try to descend inside themselves and verbalize *precisely* what they think is worrying them. His basic assumption is that "unfocused anxieties tend to spread, as if they had been injected into the psychic bloodstream. To focus them precisely causes them to retreat back to their own small localized area. We all know how a small stone in the shoe can spoil a pleasant walk or how some minor problem can keep you awake all night, generating increasing cycles of anxiety. On the other hand, when you have some agonizing itch and you scratch it, the sheer relief creates an odd sense of control and purpose, *of ceasing to be passive and becoming active*. (This, indeed, is the essence of Freud's "talking cure," but he missed its significance by getting sidetracked into his sexual obsession.)

This is the heart of the matter. Human beings keep switching back into the passive mode. And the passive mode is like a piece of laboratory gelatin used for culturing bacteria: anxieties spread and multiply. Focusing, as Maslow's young mother did, causes us to switch back into the active mode, and the problems just seem to evaporate—or at least are seen as solvable with a little effort.

I should add that another psychologist who understood all this was Pierre Janet, who called the process "funneling." I continue to believe that Janet is perhaps the greatest underrated psychologist of all time.

I would argue that the key to the next step in humanity's evolution is the clear recognition of the "two modes" and that the passive mode (what I once called the "passive fallacy") is responsible for most of our problems.

Shaw once said, "I have solved every major problem of our time, and people still go on propounding them as if they were unsolved." I suspect he was probably right. But I do not have the slightest doubt that Shaw's claim applies, in full force, to Abraham Maslow. Reading *Future Visions* has only deepened this certainty.

—COLIN WILSON

Preface

In researching Abraham Maslow's biography several years ago, I was excited to discover that he left behind many significant unpublished writings. Ever since, I have been eager to share these papers with others inspired by his unique vision of human potential and achievement. Maslow had always been an essentially intuitive and interdisciplinary thinker, and these pieces were truly wide-ranging in scope, encompassing motivational psychology, counseling and psychotherapy, managerial theory and organizational development, and even wider concerns such as politics, government, and global peace.

In editing this volume, I have selected those articles that seemed most timely and relevant for contemporary audiences. Aside from providing descriptive titles for each piece, my task has mainly involved enhancing Maslow's style for readability and correcting various errors in syntax and spelling. To place all these papers in the wider context of Maslow's evolving career, I also have written appropriate introductions and a glossary of his technical terms.

If this book sheds new light on Maslow's unpublished projects and additionally helps to reawaken interest in his important, overall legacy, my hopes will have been fulfilled.

—EDWARD HOFFMAN

Acknowledgments

The task of editing Abraham Maslow's unpublished papers has been a most enjoyable one. This volume could not have been possible without the active involvement of others. First, I wish to thank Ann Kaplan for her cooperation and enthusiasm about making her father's unpublished materials available in this format. I am grateful to Dr. Thomas Greening, longtime editor of the *Journal for Humanistic Psychology,* for his sagacious advice that I should bring this project to the attention of Sage Publications. For stimulating dialogue over the past few years pertaining to Maslow's enduring work, I wish to thank Dr. Kurt Adler, Dr. Gerald Epstein, Dr. Lawrence Epstein, Aaron Hostyk, Dr. Nels Goud, Dr. W. Edward Mann, Paul Palnik, K. Dean Stanton, Mike Robinson III, Dr. Henry Stein, Dr. John Wren-Lewis, and Alyce Tresenfeld.

Much appreciation is expressed toward the History of American Psychology Archives at the University of Akron for making my trips to the voluminous Maslow Archives there as productive, efficient, and pleasant as possible. The Association for Humanistic Psychology and the Association for Humanistic Education and Development (affiliated with the American Counseling Association) have long provided constructive forums for my writings on Maslow's legacy and related topics. The editorial support and guidance provided by Jim Nageotte at Sage Publications are very much appreciated.

For their encouragement as dedicated educators, I am grateful to my parents and brother. Above all, I would like to thank my wife, Laurel, and my children, Aaron and Jeremy, for their boundless patience and emotional support from start to finish.

Abraham Maslow
A Biographical Sketch

Perhaps more than any other American psychologist in the past half-century, Abraham Maslow has powerfully affected how we view ourselves. His provocative ideas about self-fulfillment, creativity, and well-being have influenced not only such fields as psychology and counseling but also health care, education, managerial theory, organizational development, and even theology. More broadly, Maslow's notions have helped to transform popular values about the way to lead a worthwhile life. Yet, the specific content of Maslow's vast legacy and his own odyssey remain largely unknown.

Maslow was a man with a mission. His goal was nothing less than to reverse the fashionable cynicism of our time by offering a more hopeful, inspiring, and yet realistic portrait of human personality. Though Maslow readily agreed with many aspects of the Freudian and behaviorist conceptions that had dominated most of 20th-century psychology, he ultimately rejected both approaches as offering only partial truths in their dark images of our nature.

Throughout Maslow's life, he argued that a new philosophy of humanity was needed—a veritable "new enlightenment"—to help recognize and develop our loftier capacities for aesthetics, compassion, creativity, ethics, love, spirituality, and other uniquely human traits. Without such a true portrait of human essence to guide us, Maslow consistently insisted, our society would continue to generate fragmented and ineffective—and, inadvertently, even destructive—social policies and programs, from economic planning and social welfare to criminology and the treatment of addiction.

Though Maslow stood at the pinnacle of his acclaim when he died in 1970 at the age of 62, his career had been long and his accomplishments sustained. In a sense, the fame and even adulation that he achieved during the tumultuous 1960s represented only the official recognition of an influence that had steadily grown through the decades. A warm and gentle man who affected virtually everyone he met, Maslow had the unique gift to make new—and even utopian—ideas seem possible.

Maslow himself attributed much of his moral quest in psychology—and he candidly described his entire career in such terms—to his early milieu and upbringing. Born in New York City on April 1, 1908, he was the oldest child of poor and uneducated Russian-Jewish immigrants. Three brothers and three sisters (of which one died in infancy) followed over the ensuing years.

Rose and Samuel strongly encouraged their intellectually curious "Abe" (as everyone called him) to excel academically. At the neighborhood public library in the Flatbush section of Brooklyn where the Maslows lived, Abe became a voracious reader whose heroes included the muckraking novelist Upton Sinclair and founders like Thomas Jefferson of the American Revolution. By high school age, Abe had grown into a tall, gangly youth with idealistic yearnings that attracted him to democratic socialism. Though Maslow's political views shifted later in life, he never abandoned his early humanitarian concerns and utopian longings.

Coupled with young Maslow's social idealism was a strong sense of personal inadequacy. " 'My family was a miserable family and my mother was a horrible creature,' " he caustically recalled decades later. " 'The whole thrust of my life-philosophy and all my research and theorizing . . . has its roots in a hatred for and revulsion against everything she stood for' " (Hoffman, 1988, p. 1). Samuel and Rose quarreled constantly and eventually divorced (a rare act for Jewish couples of that era) when their children had all reached adulthood. Though Abe's siblings sharply disputed his dismal descriptions of their Brooklyn home life, it seems clear that he felt lonely, shy, and unhappy throughout adolescence. Aside from reading, listening to classical music was one of the few activities that offered him pleasure.

Maslow's decision to become a psychologist was not a difficult one for him. Attending the City College of New York and Cornell University, he was initially drawn to philosophy but chose to major in psychology as a more practical, scientific way of approaching human problems. The recent writings of the behaviorist leader John B. Watson and the trenchant anthropological work *Folkways* by William Graham Sumner (1940) especially influenced undergraduate Maslow. In 1928, he excitedly transferred to the University of Wisconsin for its liberal reputation, where, as he later recalled, " 'I was off to change the world' " (Hoffman, 1988, p. 34). That same year, he married his first cousin and high school sweetheart, Bertha Goodman. A married man at the age of 20, he experienced a tremendous boost of emotional maturity and corresponding self-esteem. The two would be together for the rest of his life.

EXPERIMENTAL PSYCHOLOGY

At the University of Wisconsin, Maslow was trained as an experimental psychologist whose mentors included the behaviorist Clark Hull and the iconoclastic "body type" theorist William Sheldon. Virtually all of Maslow's professors in the small, convivial department were behaviorists who believed that meaningful theories about human nature could best be developed by studying lower animals, like white rats, in laboratory settings. Initially, Maslow subscribed to this same view. Yet, he saw behaviorism as ultimately just a new tool to serve others and subordinate to broader, humanitarian concerns. That is, Maslow was dismayed that so few academicians at Wisconsin shared his strong social conscience or burning desire for world betterment.

When young Harry Harlow joined the psychology department in 1930 to study primates, Maslow immediately became drawn to such work. He greatly enjoyed Harlow's witty company and also regarded monkeys as more appropriate research subjects than rats because of monkeys' obviously greater similarity to humans. By the early 1930s, Maslow also had become interested in the personality theories of Sigmund Freud and his Viennese archrival, Alfred Adler. In Freud's view, the sexual drive was seen to be paramount for humans, whereas Adler emphasized our drive for power or mastery. To Maslow, both perspectives had their persuasive arguments, but he questioned which was actually correct.

Because Wisconsin's psychology department permitted only animal research, Maslow contrived an elaborate study (he was Harlow's first doctoral student) that succeeded in showing that the dominance position of monkeys in their social hierarchy determined their sexual behavior—and not the other way around, as Freud might have argued. That is, the more dominant the monkey (whether male or female), the more active it was sexually. Also, the incessant heterosexual and homosexual mounting that monkeys displayed was apparently a form of dominance-submissive behavior. Maslow commented that among monkeys, " 'Sexual behavior is used as an aggressive weapon often, instead of bullying or fighting, and is to a large extent interchangeable with these latter power weapons' " (Hoffman, 1988, p. 61). Among Maslow's key findings was that dominance among monkeys typically was established by mutual gaze or visual "sizing up," rather than resorting to overt fighting. As Harlow reminisced decades later, " 'To say that [this research] was ahead of its time is an understatement of magnificent magnitude' " (Hoffman, 1988, p. 62).

From such observations, Maslow advanced an original theory of primate sexuality. He contended that within the monkey social order, there exist two distinct but related forces that culminate in sexual relations among individuals: the hormonal urge to copulate and the need to establish one's dominance with respect to overlords and subordinates. Based on these intriguing findings, Maslow planned research that might enable him to look at human sexuality, such as in marital relations, in a new way, relating to dominance.

Unfortunately, when Maslow received his doctorate in 1934, the United States was suffering in the depths of the Depression. There were virtually no academic positions available, and the anti-Semitic climate flourishing at most universities made his chances for securing a post especially difficult. Maslow's mentors at Wisconsin urged him to change his first name legally from Abraham to something less obviously Jewish, but he flatly refused. Desperate and unemployed, Maslow enrolled in Wisconsin's medical school but quit in boredom after only a few months. Stressed with financial problems, he and Bertha began arguing constantly; their marriage veered toward the rocks.

PIONEERING SEXOLOGIST

In the summer of 1935, Maslow's luck finally improved. The eminent Edward Thorndike, educational psychologist at Columbia University's Teachers College, provided Maslow with a coveted, 2-year, postdoctoral fellowship. Initially, he was eager to collaborate on Thorndike's project titled "Human Nature and the Social Order," designed "to determine the relative percentages of hereditary versus environmental influences concerning a variety of human social behaviors" (Hoffman, 1988, p. 72). But Maslow characteristically soon became bored and intellectually restless. Undoubtedly, he was more interested in pursuing his own research plans regarding human sexuality and personality. " 'I thought that working on sex was the easiest way to help mankind,' " Maslow later recalled. " 'If I could discover a way to improve the sexual life by even one percent, then I could improve the whole species' " (Hoffman, 1988, p. 69).

In a confrontation that might have ended Maslow's nascent academic career, he sent Thorndike a memo that bluntly criticized his project as poorly conceptualized. By then, Maslow was already beginning unauthorized research on human sexuality by interviewing college women in Thorndike's office without even informing him, "and everybody was scandalized" (Hoffman, 1988, p. 74).

The field of sexology was quite controversial in those days, and Thorndike was uneasy with Maslow's sexually explicit interviews and questionnaires. But Thorndike courageously allowed his protégé to continue the research unhindered. Subsequently published in several professional journals, Maslow's studies suggested that women's sexual attitudes and behaviors significantly related to their dominance-drive (what today would be called self-esteem). In essence, those with higher assertiveness tended to be more active and unconventional in their sexual tastes and behaviors. Conversely, women with low assertiveness tended to be less active sexually and more conventional in their sexual preferences. Such seminal work preceded Kinsey's famous interviews by several years but seemed to have little impact on the field at the time. Most likely, the subject of women's sexuality was just too radical for America of the 1930s. However, decades later, Maslow's sexological research was rediscovered by the feminist writer Betty Friedan and helped form the intellectual basis of her 1963 best-seller, *The Feminine Mystique* (Friedan, 1963).

TEACHER–THERAPIST

In the fall of 1937, Maslow obtained a full-time position at Brooklyn College, just a few blocks from where he had grown up in Flatbush. With his warm, witty, and gregarious style of teaching, Maslow quickly became popular among students. They dubbed him the "Frank Sinatra of Brooklyn

College," a reference to another immigrant's son who was making a name for himself in quite a different profession. Maslow often invited students to his nearby home for informal get-togethers and later pioneered in using student evaluations to help determine professorial competence.

Maslow taught courses mainly in personality theory and abnormal psychology. Relying heavily on neo-Freudian theorists like Alfred Adler and Karen Horney, he coauthored, with the émigré psychiatrist Bela Mittelman, perhaps the first U.S. college textbook in abnormal psychology. Titled *Principles of Abnormal Psychology* (Maslow & Mittelman, 1941), the well-received text helped to secure Maslow's growing reputation in the academic world.

Maslow was always grateful for the opportunity he received in those years to personally know many of Europe's leading émigré psychoanalysts and psychologists. After the Nazis seized power in early 1933, virtually all of Germany's key intellectuals fled for their lives, many settling in New York City and gaining positions at the New School for Social Research. " 'I think it's fair to say that I have had the best teachers, both formal and informal, of any person who has ever lived, just because of the historical accident of being in New York City when the very cream of European intellect was migrating away from Hitler,' " Maslow later reminisced. " 'New York City in those days was simply fantastic. There has been nothing like it since Athens. And I think I knew every one of them more or less well' " (Hoffman, 1988, p. 87). Those social scientists whom Maslow eagerly sought out included the gestalt theorists Kurt Koffka, Wolfgang Köhler, and Max Wertheimer; the psychoanalysts Alfred Adler, Erich Fromm, and Karen Horney; and the neurologist Kurt Goldstein. Of all these important psychological thinkers, Adler probably exerted the greatest influence on Maslow.

Adler had been the first major figure of the Vienna Psychoanalytic Society to break with Sigmund Freud, and the two had been bitter foes since 1911. In Adler's view, Freud had grossly overestimated the importance of sexuality in personality functioning. Stressing our innate need to overcome feelings of inferiority through mastery over the environment, Adler developed his own approach called Individual Psychology. Shifting his base of activity from Austria to the United States in the late 1920s, Adler also emphasized the importance of *social feeling*—that is, the qualities of altruism, compassion, and love—in the healthy personality. Besides offering public seminars that Maslow eagerly attended, Adler often dined privately with his much younger colleague and encouraged his evolving theories about human dominance, sexuality, and self-esteem.

Meanwhile, at Brooklyn College, Maslow was finding that many students were seeking his advice for their emotional problems. At the time, counseling and clinical psychology did not yet exist as distinct professions. It was not until Carl Rogers's pioneering work in developing nondirective counseling several years later—his landmark book *Counseling and Psychotherapy* was published in 1940—that any coherent alternative to psychoanalysis was advanced (see Rogers, 1940). Thus, relying mainly on intuition, reading, and conversations with analyst friends, Maslow offered free and informal therapeutic services to students.

This therapeutic work helped Maslow feel useful in a nonacademic way. But it also had a profound effect on his emerging theory of motivation and human nature. He increasingly saw the classic Freudian view as inadequate to explain our deepest impulses and begin to posit that " 'Any talent, any capacity [is] also a motivation, a need, an impulse' " (Hoffman, 1988, p. 145).

As a counselor, Maslow typically recommended a variety of day-to-day activities to help students cope with stress. He valued dancing as a healthful and sociable way to let go of bodily and emotional tension. He also suggested that involvement in a creative activity like art or music could be uplifting and calming. For those who did not feel talented in either realm, he advised that simply listening to music or going to an art museum could be mildly therapeutic. But most important, Maslow came to believe that every individual needs to feel a sense of creative fulfillment in daily life of truly using his or her inborn talents.

During the same period, Maslow was becoming quite friendly at Columbia University with several of its leading anthropologists, including Ruth Benedict, Ralph Linton, and Margaret Mead. It may seem surprising that Maslow, trained as an experimental psychologist, was interested in anthropological issues, but he had already published a pertinent chapter titled "Personality and Patterns of Culture" in Ross Stagner's (1937) anthology, *Psychology of Personality*. In this chapter, Maslow (1937) embraced the tenets of cultural relativism: Every culture is unique, all values and mores are relative, and no culture, therefore, can judge as better its own values, much less seek to impose them on another culture.

Maslow soon came to reject this viewpoint sharply for the rest of his life, but at the time, it was associated with racial tolerance and progressive thinking. To most social scientists, the alternative seemed to be a return to the outmoded concept of the "white man's burden," which had given 19th-century Western colonialism its moral justification. In this same essay, Maslow also affirmed the hope that science would some day furnish a new set of values—

replacing those of traditional religion—to promote the well-being of all peoples. Such would remain Maslow's core belief throughout his career.

In the summer of 1938, Maslow undertook cross-cultural fieldwork under Ruth Benedict's supervision. Anxiously leaving behind in Brooklyn his wife Bertha and their newborn baby, Ann, he lived with two colleagues on a Canadian reservation housing the Northern Blackfoot Indian tribe. The experience lasted only a summer, but it changed Maslow's life and ensuing career. " 'As things stood while I was studying anthropology in 1933–1937, cultures were unique, idiosyncratic. There was no scientific way of handling them, no generalizations that you could make,' " he later recollected. " 'The first and foremost lesson that [I] learned . . . was that Indians are first of all people, individuals, human beings, and only secondarily Blackfoot Indians. By comparison with similarities, the differences, though undoubtedly there, seemed superficial' " (Hoffman, 1988, p. 111).

Maslow's exposure to the Blackfoot tribe was truly a transformative experience. For one thing, it was his first exposure to a different culture, and it helped him to shed the ethnocentric bias held almost reflexively by most U.S. academic psychologists. For another, he was very much affected by the cooperativeness, noncompetitiveness, and sharing that Blackfoot individuals showed—admirable qualities that seemed woefully lacking in mainstream North American culture.

Maslow later recalled,

"I came into the reservation with the notion that the Indians are over there on a shelf, like a butterfly collection or something like that. And then slowly I shifted and changed my mind. Those Indians on the reservation were decent people, and the more I got to know the whites in the village, who were the worst bunch of creeps and bastards I'd ever run across in my life, the more it got paradoxical. Which was the asylum? Who were the keepers and who the inmates? Everything got all mixed up." (Hoffman, 1988, p. 119)

Maslow discovered that fundamental to the Blackfoot, and to Plains Native Americans in general, was a marked emphasis on generosity as the highest virtue. To most Blackfoot members, wealth was not important in terms of accumulating property and possessions: *giving it away* was what brought one the true status of prestige and security in the tribe. Through Blackfoot eyes, the wealthiest individual was the one who had given away the most to others—not merely in one big display of generosity, but in continuous demonstration. With Maslow's strong socialist sensibility, this altruistic and moralistic outlook on wealth was quite appealing.

By the time Maslow had returned to Brooklyn, he was already conceptualizing a new biologically rooted but humanistic approach to personality transcending the narrowness of cultural relativism. Thus, in a summary report to the Social Science Research Council several weeks after his fieldwork, he explained that

> "It would seem that every human being comes at birth into society not as a lump of clay to be molded by society, but rather as a structure which society may warp or suppress or build upon. . . . I am now struggling with a notion of a 'fundamental' [or] 'natural' personality structure." (Hoffman, 1988, p. 128)

MOTIVATIONAL THEORY
AND THE QUEST FOR PEACE

Maslow's experience with the Blackfoot tribe convinced him that humane alternatives to mainstream Western society could actually exist. He became especially interested in conceptualizing new social institutions so that people might feel less isolated from one another and, hence, more emotionally secure. But then came the onset of World War II, and in late 1941, Maslow decided that understanding human motivation would be his lifelong contribution to the world:

> "One day just after Pearl Harbor, I was driving home and my car was stopped by a poor, pathetic parade. . . . As I watched, the tears began to run down my face. I felt that we didn't understand—not Hitler, nor the Germans, nor Stalin, nor the Communists. I felt that if we could understand, then we could make progress. I had a vision of a peace table, with people sitting around it, talking about human nature and hatred and peace and brotherhood. . . . I realized that the rest of my life must be devoted to discovering a psychology for the peace table." (Hoffman, 1988, p. 148)

During the next few years, Maslow was extremely productive. He developed his famous *hierarchy of needs* and the concept of *self-actualization* as our highest motivating force. Maslow was aware that he had ventured into unknown territory of the mind and that no one in the psychology field was attempting to synthesize all known theoretical approaches in this bold manner. In essence, Maslow postulated that every person is born with certain *basic needs* encompassing the physiological, including needs for safety, belongingness or love, and self-esteem. He argued that these basic needs can be seen as making up an unfolding hierarchy:

> "It is quite true that man lives by bread alone—when there is no bread. But what happens to man's desires when there is plenty of bread and his belly is chronically filled? At once other (and 'higher') needs emerge, and these, rather than physiological hungers, dominate the organism. And when these in turn are satisfied, again new (and still 'higher') needs emerge, and so on." (Hoffman, 1988, p. 154)

One of Maslow's greatest conceptual achievements in mid-career was that of self-actualization. Initially based on his personal acquaintance with Ruth Benedict and Max Wertheimer, Maslow became curious and then intensely driven to understand the motivations of such highly successful yet socially concerned people. Eventually, he was sure that none of the classic Freudian or neo-Freudian approaches were adequate. Maslow contended,

> "A musician must make music, an artist must paint, a poet must write, if he is to be ultimately at peace with himself. What a man can be, he must be. This need we may call self-actualization. . . . It refers to man's desire for self-fulfillment, namely, to the tendency for him to become actually in what he is potentially: to become everything that one is capable of becoming." (Hoffman, 1988, p. 155)

Maslow was tremendously excited by the new vistas of the mind that he was glimpsing. He became certain that psychology can best learn about higher motivations by studying emotionally healthy people. No amount of animalistic research or psychiatric work with the severely disturbed could provide this knowledge, argued Maslow. For this reason, he began reading about history's acclaimed saints, sages, and scientists to look for commonalities in their outlook and behavior. As a social scientist who always had been antagonistic toward religion, he found it hard to shift intellectual gears in this way. But Maslow felt strongly that he was on the right track, no matter what his more conventional colleagues were saying.

In this context, Maslow wrote the following statement:

> "If we want to answer the question, how tall can the human species grow, then obviously it is well to pick out the ones who are already tallest and study them. If we want to know how fast a human being can run, then it is no use to average out the speed of the population; it is far better to collect Olympic gold medal

winners and see how well they can do. If we want to know the possibilities for spiritual growth, value growth, or moral development in human beings, then I maintain that we can learn most by studying our most moral, ethical, or saintly people." (Hoffman, 1988, p. 185)

Suddenly, in the mid-1940s, Maslow was stricken with a mysterious and devastating illness. He was forced to take medical leave from Brooklyn College for several years and moved out to rural Pleasanton, California, with Bertha and their two children, Ann and Ellen. There, at a branch of the Maslow Cooperage, Abe's brothers generously supported his family and gave him an easy managerial post supervising the repair of wooden barrels used by the nearby wineries. Eventually, his health improved to normal, and his brothers, impressed with Abe's outgoing personality and sales ability, offered him a permanent partnership with the successful company. Longing to resume college teaching and research, Abe graciously declined the offer. But his practical, day-to-day lessons at the Maslow Cooperage played an important role in his subsequent managerial theorizing.

Not long after returning to Brooklyn College, in 1951, Maslow obtained a position heading the psychology department at newly established Brandeis University near Boston. It was an exciting opportunity, for at the relatively youthful academic age of 43, he would have sizable impact in forming an entire faculty. At Brooklyn College, Maslow had long felt professionally isolated among experimentalist colleagues and burdened by the heavy teaching load. Now, he was delighted to be among fellow scholars in the humanities and social sciences who shared his broad interests.

It was in 1954 that Maslow wrote *Motivation and Personality,* a brilliant and far-reaching text. It was a synthesis of nearly 15 years of theorizing about human nature, and it immediately catapulted him to international prominence. His tone was bold and confident:

The science of psychology has been far more successful on the negative than on the positive side. . . . It has revealed to us much about man's shortcomings, his illnesses, his sins, but little about his potentialities, his virtues, his achievable aspirations or his psychological health. . . . We must find out what psychology might be if it could free itself from the stultifying effects of limited, pessimistic and stingy preoccupations with human nature. (Maslow, 1954, p. 354)

Maslow also recommended in *Motivation and Personality* a host of new research projects based on its underlying viewpoint. Maslow observed,

We spend a great amount of time studying criminality. Why not study law-abidingness, identification with society, social conscience? . . . In addition to studying the [therapeutic] effects of . . . good life experiences, such as marriage, having children, falling in love [and] education, we should also study the [therapeutic] effects of bad experiences, particularly of tragedy, but also illness, deprivation, frustration, and the like. Healthy people seem able to turn even such experiences to good use. (Maslow, 1954, p. 371)

The book was widely acknowledged as a major psychological achievement of the 1950s. Its ideas—particularly the hierarchy of inborn needs and self-actualization—began to exert a powerful impact on the budding field of counseling. Together with a few names of like-minded colleagues like Gordon Allport, Erich Fromm, Rollo May, and Carl Rogers, Maslow's name began to stand for an innovative and optimistic approach to human nature. Their central tenet was the concept of personality growth, which continues long after bodily growth has ceased in late adolescence. By the early 1960s, such theorists became known as the leaders of a new movement called *humanistic psychology* or the *Third Force* (in relation to the earlier two movements of psychoanalysis and behaviorism).

PEAK-EXPERIENCES AND SPIRITUALITY

Since first studying the lives of history's self-actualizing people, Maslow had been intrigued that many had reported mystical-like episodes. Always skeptical toward religion, he initially turned his attention to other matters. But during the mid-1950s, this finding seemed so consistent and enigmatic that Maslow felt obliged to pursue it. He began interviewing college students and others and discovered with astonishment that many had undergone moments of great rapture and meaning during daily life. The "trigger" for such events seemed to vary tremendously—from a leisurely walk on a sunny spring day to listening to captivating music. But strikingly, the words that such persons used to describe their blissful episodes were precisely those favored by famous mystics throughout history.

In a professional paper presented in 1956, Maslow dubbed these moments of ecstasy *peak-experiences* and suggested that they were a key to our unrealized, inner potential (see Maslow, 1959). He described nearly 20 common features of the peak-experience, which he associated with extreme inner health. Based on his sample's phenomenological reports, these included temporary disorientation with respect to time and space, feelings of wonder and awe, great happiness, and a complete, though momentary, loss of fear and defense before the grandeur of the universe. People typically mentioned that polar opposites, like good and evil, free will and destiny, seemed transcended in such instants: Everything was connected to everything else in a unity of splendor.

Finally, perhaps constituting the most important aspect of his paper, Maslow noted that peak-experiences often leave profound and transformative effects in their wake. " 'Generally, the person is more apt to feel that life . . . is worthwhile, even if it is usually drab, pedestrian, painful, or ungratifying, since beauty, truth, and meaningfulness have been demonstrated . . . to exist' " (Hoffman, 1988, p. 226). Perhaps forgetting about the seminal work of William James, Maslow argued that such experiences are " 'plentifully recorded in human history, but so far as I know have never received the attention of psychologists or psychiatrists' " (Hoffman, 1988, p. 226).

Over the next few years, Maslow extended his theoretical outlook. He suggested that during transcendental moments, people directly apprehend humanity's highest virtues and ideals—what he termed *Being-values*—like beauty, justice, and completion. In contrast, our mundane existence is dominated by lesser, *Deficiency-values* such as fear or suspicion. He also speculated that emotionally healthy persons are more likely to undergo ecstatic, mystical-like experiences than those struggling with inner conflicts. Such formulations exerted an influence far beyond academia.

Undoubtedly, the catalyst was Maslow's (1962/1968b) book, *Toward a Psychology of Being*. A collection of his essays and addresses over the preceding 8 years, it became extremely popular, eventually selling 200,000 copies before a trade edition was issued in 1968. The book opened on a stirring note:

> Every age but ours has its model, its hero. All of these have been given to us by our culture: the hero, the gentleman, the knight, the mystic. About all we have left is the well-adjusted man without problems, a very pale and doubtful substitute. Perhaps we shall soon be able to use as our guide and model the fully growing and self-fulfilling human, the one in whom his potentialities are coming to full development, the one whose inner nature expresses itself freely, rather than being warped, repressed, or denied. (p. 5)

Toward a Psychology of Being was the kind of book passed around from person to person, a book that not only inspires but changes people's lives. Many more were affected by its message than actually read it. Terms like self-actualization and peak-experience began to penetrate the popular English language and help shape the mood of the 1960s. Before long, nearly every college student in the United States was hearing such phrases, as legions of admirers promoted Maslow's perspective.

In Maslow's final years, he advanced a new outlook that he called *transpersonal psychology*—focusing on spirituality and "the farthest reaches of human nature." He was a key figure in launching this nascent discipline, for he felt that humanistic psychology was inadequately dealing with spiritual concerns. He observed,

"[Humanistic psychology] is like Sweden, Norway, and Denmark, where God died and there *is* no god, where everything is sensible, rational, commonsensical, logical, empirical but not yet transcendent. You can admire and respect Scandinavia, but you can't love it, much less worship it! Everything that a good, mundane, this-worldly reasonable intelligence could do has been done there. But it's not enough!" (Hoffman, 1988, p. 282)

Maslow's groundbreaking work on peak-experiences and exotic mental states like meditation helped bring about a sudden scientific respectability to the study of mysticism. Not since William James at the turn of the 20th century had North American psychology shown a sympathetic interest in religious experience. In 1964, Maslow's book *Religions, Values, and Peak-Experiences* was published to wide acclaim. Placing the peak-experience at the center of spirituality, he argued that these rare, transcendent episodes were the "core" of all authentic religion and also had important healing potential:

The power of the peak-experience could permanently affect [our] attitude toward life. A single glimpse of heaven is enough to confirm its existence even if it is never experienced again. It is my strong suspicion that one such experience might be able to prevent suicide . . . and perhaps many varieties of slow self-destruction, such as alcoholism, drug-addiction, and addiction to violence. (Maslow, 1964, p. 75)

FOUNDER OF
ENLIGHTENED MANAGEMENT

Maslow's optimistic approach to human personality and motivation also attracted many in the budding field of managerial theory. Among them was Douglas McGregor, a professor at the Massachusetts Institute of Technology.

His landmark book, *The Human Side of Enterprise,* published in 1960, high-lighted two distinct managerial styles: Theory X, which views people as inherently lazy and selfish, and Theory Y, which regards them as innately productive and cooperative. In outlining Theory Y, McGregor (1960) clearly subscribed to Maslow's view of human nature.

Shortly thereafter, Maslow was asked to observe a real-life testing of his theories at Non-Linear Systems, a high-tech company based in southern California. Its owner-entrepreneur had organized his work environment around Theory Y principles. Employee creativity, cooperation, and self-direction were encouraged as much as possible. There was a strong emphasis on em-ployee training and skill-growth and even a "vice president for innovation."

During his stay at Non-Linear Systems, Maslow recorded his observations as well as his reactions to existing managerial books he was reading. Gradu-ally a manuscript took form, its subjects ranging from methods of enhancing employee motivation to team decision making and the psychology of lead-ership. He also discussed some of his own experiences as plant manager and salesperson for the Maslow Cooperage in Pleasanton, California. Perhaps most significantly, he elaborated on the concept of *synergy,* which anthro-pologist Ruth Benedict originally had used in unpublished lectures in 1941, to refer to cultures in which cooperation is rewarded and advantageous to all.

Benedict's notion was almost unknown except to Maslow, Margaret Mead, and a handful of others who had known her personally. Now Maslow saw synergy as an underlying principle of management and human relation-ships in organizations. Non-Linear Systems seemed to be clearly demonstrat-ing that the company's and the employee's interests could converge through what Maslow called *enlightened management.*

This manuscript was published as *Eupsychian Management* (Maslow, 1965) (*eupsychia* was his term for the ideal society or organization). Despite its formidable title, the book brought Maslow praise from North American leaders in management education and training and eventually those in Japan as well. Many consulting offers came his way. Though gratified by the re-sponse, Maslow remained realistic about business—perhaps more so than some of his admirers. He realized that the humanistic approach depends partly on good conditions and that a sudden downturn in the international economy or domestic markets might make the principles of enlightened man-agement less tenable.

In the 5 years between *Eupsychian Management* and his sudden death in 1970, Maslow enjoyed international renown as the founder of the rapidly growing movement to humanize the workplace. He was elected president of the American Psychological Association in 1966 and then began developing a new theoretical concept: the Theory Z approach to management. In essence, Maslow contended that neither Theory X nor Theory Y as McGregor had described them is really correct. Rather, as people grow toward self-actualization, their psychological needs at work undergo a corresponding change. For example, salary increases alone rarely mean much to those propelled by higher needs—what Maslow called the *metaneeds* for creativity, novelty, autonomy, and self-expression. He was sure that the North American workplace was steadily changing to recognize this facet of human personality and motivation.

After suffering a major heart attack in late 1967, Maslow had a sense that his life would not be long. Nevertheless, he refused to slow down significantly and continued to sustain a hectic pace of writing, lecturing, and consulting. With a sense of urgency about the importance of his humanistic work for world improvement and peace, Maslow viewed even semiretirement as unthinkable. However, he took a medical leave from Brandeis University to accept a generous 4-year fellowship funded by the founder-owner of the California-based Saga Corporation near Palo Alto.

Maslow relocated from the Boston area in early 1969, and his final months were happy and productive. He and Bertha socialized actively. Though lacking the stamina for undertaking any major projects, Maslow was busily dictating notes on a host of theoretical and applied topics pertaining to his far-flung career interests. At times, he hoped that his health would improve sufficiently to allow extensive travel abroad for new cross-cultural research. But such was not to be. In June 1970, Maslow died at his home from a massive heart attack, leaving behind many unfinished papers and plans.

PART I

Personality, Growth, and Therapy

Among Maslow's many contributions to psychology and wider social science has been his emphasis on how human motivation and personality are affected by cultural factors. Especially influenced by anthropologist Ruth Benedict at Columbia University whom he knew personally, Maslow in later life articulated the concepts of synergy and eupsychia in discussing how individual personality and culture are always closely intertwined. This brief, unpublished paper was written on June 4, 1970, 4 days before Maslow suddenly succumbed to heart disease. In it, he indicated some of his most important intellectual influences in this interdisciplinary field.

1

My Early Revelations
About Culture and Personality

The more I think of the *eupsychian* society, the more I realize how profoundly I was affected by the social anthropology I discovered at the University of Wisconsin about 1932. It was when I first began to read Bronislaw Malinowski, Margaret Mead, Ruth Benedict, and Ralph Linton. For me, this was all a tremendous revelation, and I went around lecturing to the psychology classes of various instructors about this new dispensation for our field. I was convinced that psychology had been badly ethnocentric. I decided for myself to be a part-time anthropologist because that seemed to be sine qua non for being a good psychologist. Otherwise, you were simply a naive local. And I remember lecturing everybody else about it too.

It was during this time that I also researched and wrote what was probably the first essay on personality and culture by any psychologist in the United

States. It was a chapter for Ross Stagner's (1937) textbook *Psychology of Personality.* I had written a huge quantity of material several years before the volume was issued, and my chapter for Stagner was very much a condensation (see Maslow, 1937).

My revelation in Wisconsin about psychology and culture was a successor to the one that I had experienced during my sophomore year at New York's City College. That one occurred when I read William Graham Sumner's (1940) book *Folkways.* I had stumbled across the book by the sheerest accident. It came about because I had registered for a course titled Philosophy of Civilization to be taught by Professor Morris Raphael Cohen, whom I had very much admired and with whom I had wanted to study. When I showed up in class, I learned that Cohen was off on a sabbatical and Professor Scott Buchanan instead was taking his place. He assigned *Folkways* as the prime textbook for the course.

I never did discover what the hell Buchanan was talking about. Partly, it was too difficult for me; I just wasn't educated enough back then. But partly, also, he is a chaotic thinker (I now know) and I still don't know what the hell Buchanan is talking about. In any case, at that time, I blamed my difficulty on myself and dropped out of the course. Because I became fascinated with Sumner's work, however, this was probably one of the most important courses I ever took.

I nibbled away at *Folkways,* not quite understanding it. I kept coming back to it, again and again. Then, one night when I was all alone in the furniture place at which I was working part-time as a night watchman, I experienced while reading *Folkways* a big breakthrough of awe and admiration. It was a kind of cold chill and hair-standing-on-end *peak-experience.* I was not merely happy; I also felt a sense of the uncanny and of littleness, incapability, and the like.

The point is that my vow—that's what it would have been called 500 years ago—was also a resolution: to do like Sumner. I swore that I would try to make a similar contribution to philosophy, psychology, and anthropology. Why these three particular fields, I don't remember. But that evening, my ethnocentrism dropped away like old clothes, and I became a citizen of the world.

If I had been in King Arthur's court, I suppose that I would have kept vigil beside my sword and before an altar all night long. That was exactly the spirit of it. In any case, that's what I've done with my life.

Abraham Maslow is well-known for his emphasis on emotional health rather than pathology as the appropriate basis for personality study. In using this approach, he always sought to find concrete examples from everyday life. In this unpublished essay written in November 1964, Maslow sought to shed new light on everyone's primary concern, namely, happiness.

2

The Psychology of Happiness

It is time to jettison the conventional, hedonistic definition of happiness as simply a state of pleasure without pain. That is, we must redefine and enrich the concept of happiness. My main point is that the subject of high and low "grumbles"—complaints—is vital to this whole discussion. The English author Colin Wilson (1959, 1964) has called this concept the "Saint Neot's margin" or the "margin of indifference."

The problem with our normative definition of happiness is that we are often psychologically unaware of our present good fortune. This truism raises the question: Can we be happy if we're not consciously aware of it? Are we happy only in retrospect, which is often the case, when during present bad fortune we retrospectively appreciate our former good luck and then only realize that we were happy? This too creates a problem in definition: Can we legitimately define happiness in retrospective terms?

We must redefine happiness to include the good fortune we take for granted and that may, therefore, lapse from daily awareness. It also seems useful to learn specific inner techniques to bring this outlook into conscious awareness so that we can appreciate our blessings rather than take them for granted.

In general, our experience of pain is certainly prepotent over pleasure. But it is equally important to consider that pains, deprivations, complaints, frustrations, and grumbles force their way into consciousness far more readily than do our gratifications. An important issue to consider is that with familiarity, our gratifications lose their "peak" or wondrous qualities, gradually dissipate, and then fade into preconsciousness. For instance, this phenomenon has been true for musical enjoyment in my life.

Though real happiness may be transient, it is still quite vivid in memory and can be deliberately recalled, reexperienced, and reenjoyed like a ruminated cud. This involves a voluntary and intellectual process that we can all learn to accomplish. It is also a way to widen and enrich our ordinary consciousness.

BEYOND HEDONISM

I am convinced that the hedonistic definition of happiness is false, for real happiness necessarily implies difficulties. For example, it is a privilege to undergo the "misery" of creativity, even the related insomnia and tension. It is a privilege to have children to weep over because of their troubles, rather than to have no children at all. It is a privilege to love family members and friends, even though doing so inevitably means to suffer all their pain in addition to your own. Indeed, this situation is infinitely better than the misery of being wholly alone in life. We must, therefore, define "good living" and happiness to include these "misery privileges."

For instance, Beethoven was tortured over his music. Yet, who wouldn't want to be a Beethoven? Or, more broadly, who would renounce the privilege of creating eternal music due to the transitory pain of creativity? After all, it is possible to avoid all problems in life, to live a cowlike existence of tranquillity and peace without sweat of any kind. This can be easily accomplished by having a prefrontal lobotomy or by perpetually ingesting alcohol, narcotics, or tranquilizers.

Thus, we must learn to enjoy the "miseries of the higher life" and of creativity, or *real* problems rather than pseudoproblems. Is this possible? I think so, for if we place these problems in the widest gestalt of our former, present, and future life span, and if we juxtapose them in comparison with the problems of other people and from the perspective of the entire cosmos, then our real problems acquire their appropriate place and it becomes possible to experience the paradox of enjoying the miseries of the higher life. Life isn't really life without these anyway. Empty sleep and dullness are not living.

In my view, human nature always involves seeking better and better heavens. We must abandon our expectation of never-ending contentment and serenity, for such peak feelings can come only from transient episodes. For instance, consider the risks entailed in having a baby. Of course, we will worry about it beforehand. After all, the baby might be born handicapped, sick, or stillborn. Then the question is legitimately raised: "Why buy this misery?"

The same issue is true for falling in love and for getting married. "Why buy problems?" "Why buy trouble?" I think that such an attitude can be demonstrated as self-deluding and a sure path toward unhappiness in life.

I think it can be shown psychologically that self-actualizing people gladly accept such "troubles" and that such troubles are actually wonderful in comparison to the real miseries of boredom, loneliness, and the experientially empty and stultified life. The state of feeling empty inside is worse than experiencing the complexities of friendship and love, which may indeed bring miseries.

I once counseled a distressed teenager who said, "If I had been hit by that car, my problems would have all been over! They would have ended right then and there. Maybe that would have been better!" But then think of all the lovely problems that youngster would have missed, all the pleasant "tortures" of life. To worry over something worthwhile is certainly better than not having anything or anyone to worry about at all.

For example, to worry about something outside of yourself means to forget the self. This is itself a pleasant state of consciousness. Not having anything outside yourself to arouse your interest, excitement, or worry means that you are dumped right in the lap of your own self-consciousness, which can be the most miserable emotional state.

Perhaps we should, therefore, redefine happiness as *experiencing real emotions over real problems and real tasks.*

Apparently, the act of seeking directly for happiness just does not work psychologically as a means of living a worthwhile life. Instead, happiness may actually be a by-product, an epiphenomenon, of something that comes en passant. The best way to realize retrospectively that you were happy, even though you lacked awareness at the time, is to be committed to a worthy task or cause and to work in a dedicated way for it.

Another example that my research has uncovered is the "worthwhile" pain that some women experience during natural childbirth. One woman reported that her pain was "good," because it was related to a good cause: It would give her the baby she wanted. It also meant that she was giving birth rather than the obstetrician. It was her accomplishment, her pride.

What did this attitude indicate, then, about the woman's very real and excruciating physical pain? That it should not be regarded purely negatively as only pain. The question, therefore, becomes: In what cause is the pain enlisted? Is it a worthwhile pain?

Another example comes to mind. My colleague David served in the Marines during World War II. One night as he sat cold and shivering in a wet foxhole, he experienced a kind of illumination about the meaning of it all. Instead of fixing his gaze on the displeasurable, concrete moment and place, he was suddenly able to place his military involvement in a larger context and gestalt: to see his physical discomfort as a worthwhile and even dignified means to a very significant end. He actually gained a thrill and relived the excitement of patriotism.

Still another example is of the tough prizefighter who is proud to be punched just to show that he can "take it." He will offer you his belly, say "Hit as hard as you can," and then smile with pride to show that it didn't hurt. Indeed, one can even be proud of scars if these are won in an honorable battle. Pregnancy striations and scars on the belly can be of this sort. They can be viewed very romantically and symbolically as a sign of something wonderful and honorable, akin to making one "qualified" for membership in a coveted club. One's scars both literally and symbolically are qualifiers, and therefore, one can be very proud of them.

Finally, I have heard many older mothers say with regret and nostalgia as they watch others' little children play, "I wish I had sense enough to enjoy my children while they were still young and cute, instead of getting so bothered by the moment-to-moment, day-to-day irritations. Now, I realize how cute they were and how much I could have enjoyed myself!"

To ponder this viewpoint brings us to an additional perspective on the happiness question. Why? Because it suggests that we should ideally see the present activity against a wider backdrop, as *figure against ground.* Such mothers who fretted and worried continually over their young children instead of enjoying them were, in a certain sense, reduced to the concrete. What they should have done was to adopt a time-gestalt perspective: to recognize that their little ones would one day grow up. These parents also should have had the general, preconscious awareness that having cute children is a great privilege and a great good fortune and that it is possible not to have *any* children.

From infertile couples, we learn how miserable that state of affairs can actually be. After unsuccessfully trying to conceive, such couples can become incredibly appreciative of the existence of babies. Oftentimes, these couples will overcome the most tremendous difficulties to adopt a child, that is, to "buy" all the troubles and nuisances of child rearing. This example certainly indicates that we can sometimes fully appreciate a gratification because we've first experienced a period of frustration and yearning.

All of these thoughts suggest that happiness is a lot more complicated than its conventional, hedonistic definition as merely the absence of pain. It is time for a whole new psychological approach.

Throughout Abraham Maslow's life, he prided himself as a scientist and an empirically based thinker about human nature. He completely rejected the acceptance of psychological notions that seemed attractive but ultimately lacked validation. So too with Maslow's own theory of self-actualization. In this unpublished paper written in October 1966, he sought to make explicit some of humanistic psychology's unproven assumptions, axioms, and beliefs.

3

Critique of Self-Actualization Theory

For several years, I have felt that humanistic psychology's tacit assumptions should be dragged out into the open and that an astute philosopher could legitimately raise questions about these unproven beliefs. In this paper, I would like to critique several features of humanistic psychology and its particular axioms.

First, it should be made clear that the entire model of humanistic psychology and *self-actualization* rests on the assumption that the person wants to live. When an individual's death-wishes are strong, the whole psychological system falls to the ground. Thus, there are apparently no intrinsically self-validating and end experiences of the *peak-experience* type to which we could point as making life worthwhile. In short, when life is judged as not worthwhile—whether through the accumulation of pains or the absence of peak-experiences and positive joys—then humanistic psychology is worthless. It speaks only to those people who want to live and grow, become happier and more effective, fulfill themselves, like themselves better, improve in general, and move toward the ideal of perfection, even though t. never expect to fully reach that point.

Second, humanistic psychology assumes that there is a definite human essence, at least, *some* fixity of human nature. The specific form that this takes is, of course, the theory of instincts. But it is also the theory of capacity and needs, that is, the very fact of capacities "wanting" to express and fulfill themselves. This model is a complete rejection of Jean-Paul Sartre's concept of total and ultimate relativity and of the radical, arbitrary existentialism that he embraces. In contrast, I believe that human nature is *not* infinitely malleable and has definite parameters.

A third assumption of self-actualization theory is that it very strongly requires a pluralism of individual differences. This requires that we accept hereditary, constitutional, and temperamental differences—and do so in a joyful rather than grudging way. Such a true acceptance of individual differences has several key implications that should be stated briefly.

Among these notions is the "horticulture" rather than the "sculpture" model of personality growth. Whether in the domain of psychotherapy, counseling, education, or family life, this model should guide us. It means that we try to make a rose into a good rose, rather than seek to change roses into lilies. It implies a kind of Taoism, an acceptance of what people really are; it necessitates a pleasure in the self-actualization of a person who may be quite different from yourself. It even implies an ultimate respect and acknowledgment of the sacredness and uniqueness of each kind of person.

For instance, I recently visited the University of Rhode Island and became involved in a discussion with their psychology faculty. I made a severe attack on their single-minded conception of the Ph.D.—as if there were just one kind of Ph.D. or as if there were just one standard model. I pointed out that many different kinds of talents exist and that certainly we need these varieties of skills. With the monolithic Ph.D. model that American psychology departments embrace, perhaps 90% of potential psychologists are screened out. Our so-called high standards of acceptance are really techniques for rejecting the vast majority of interested young people who should become psychologists.

For graduate psychology departments to base admission solely on statistical and experimental prowess is as logical as valuing only those students who have blue eyes or good gallbladders. It is a situation like that of classical China, in which emperors filled all governmental positions with persons who were evaluated solely according to their skill in calligraphy.

In another context, I have already made the point of how you train someone to become a good prizefighter. That is, the trainer sees what the individual's natural style is like and then tries to make him into a better model of *that particular style*—not to make him conform to a generalized, abstract exemplar of prize fighting.

In short, humanistic psychology involves an acceptance of people as they are at their intrinsic core and then regards therapists as simply Taoist helpers for them. We strive to enable people to become healthy and effective *in their own style*.

A fourth topic that should be addressed explicitly is whether we have merely incorporated into self-actualization theory traditional Judeo-Christian values in evaluating the emotional health of individuals. In this vein, I often have been accused of describing people as self-actualizing according to whether I find them "likable" or not.

My response has been that the model of self-actualization so far seems not only cross-cultural but even cross-historical as well. In cultures as diverse as the Japanese and Blackfoot Native American, I have found significant similarities in how the saint or sage is depicted. Nevertheless, it is possible that I have fallen victim to sampling error and of projecting my own values into my research. This issue must be treated with great seriousness.

A fifth axiom of self-actualization theory is my contention—as yet unproven—that neurosis must be considered as a psychological defense and not basic to human nature. Furthermore, neurosis must be viewed as a defense against the authentic self, our deeper layers, full humanness, growth, and self-actualization.

From this assumption, I have argued vigorously that effective counseling and psychotherapy are Taoistic and uncovering rather than involving mainly shaping, molding, or indoctrinating. Of course, pure Taoism is impossible in principle. Yet effective counselors and therapists move far in this direction. They really respect the other person's inner core and regard themselves as obstetricians, horticulturists, or midwives who simply help the person give birth to himself or herself and help him or her grow, *in his or her own style,* toward self-fulfillment.

Interestingly, the positive human traits are all strengthened and confirmed by uncovering and insight. These include the qualities of self-respect, of security and safety, of being lovable, of being able to love someone else, and of being aware of the need to be loved and to love. Conversely, negative human traits like cruelty, sadism, or masochism are destroyed by successful

Taoistic, uncovering kinds of counseling and psychotherapy. Indeed, this evidence is a key reason for regarding the former qualities as intrinsic aspects of humanness and the latter as reactive and sick.

It may be relevant to observe here that ordinary neurosis and even the *value pathologies* like delinquency may consequently be viewed as efforts toward the gratification of basic needs and *metaneeds* but under the conditions of anxiety, fear, and lack of courage.

A sixth point is that in any discussion of self-actualization, there arises my requirement that people must have a choice of values and that if they do, they will prefer the *Being-values* over neurotic values. Of course, this statement immediately raises the issue of having "good conditions." This means several things. Most immediately, it means good conditions for choosing—which necessitates full access to information, to the truth. Useful information must not be hidden. This notion applies to undemocratic governments that censor the news or give out slanted news. It also applies to the one-newspaper town in our country or to corporations or labor unions that act as monopolies. It also means being able to choose without fear or social pressure.

Yet, I also must take into account the concept of the "good chooser" or at least the "reasonably good specimen." I often find myself talking about zookeepers wanting a "good, tigerish tiger" or a "good, equine horse." Zookeepers and zoologists have no difficulty with such concepts and simply take them for granted. Only philosophy professors boggle at the concept. Ultimately, if I write this systematically, I must focus on the whole question of what the human species *tries to get away from* and what the human species *moves toward*. From such a perspective, it seems clear that people move toward self-actualization.

Seventh, I must accept very frankly as a thus-far insoluble problem the present impossibility of distinguishing objectively between a healthy peak-experience and a manic-attack. It is quite true that I can talk about the phenomenology showing that manic-attacks mask desperation, fear, and depression. But that's not really a convincing, objective truth to someone who refuses to accept the outlook of humanistic psychology. To some extent, the same difficulty exists in distinguishing a healthy peak from a neurotic or psychotic peak. Until we have better techniques of phenomenology and personality assessment, this issue remains one of the weak spots of the entire system of humanistic psychology.

I am, therefore, finding it necessary to build into the system not only the existence of peak-experiences but also some method of confirming or validating these peaks to distinguish the true from the false. Essentially, this means a follow-up of the individual. Specifically, it introduces the variable of time. It also introduces the concept of validating peaks by what *subsequently* happens to the person. For example, it now appears that the psychedelic experience is less and less desirable for the individual as time goes by. This kind of chemically induced peak does not hold up as well as the "natural" peak-experience.

A fancy way of saying all this is that the normal equipment of science must be invoked and considered absolutely necessary, because all inspirations, illuminations, peaks, and insights need to be externally validated, verified, and confirmed. Currently, the only way we know how to accomplish this task is to examine what occurs after the illumination and to check and recheck it. This notion can even be phrased in the old religious way: "How does one distinguish whether the inner voices are of God or the devil?" The answer is to see pragmatically what happens to the person in later time.

Eighth, in such discussions, I find that eventually the question of *method* arises. That is, weren't my choices of secure versus insecure individuals merely a reflection of my own values? Didn't I choose my self-actualization subjects on a personal basis? Am I not building my own values into the theory of self-actualization?

One answer that I find necessary is that it is perfectly true that I must start with my own intuition and faith in my own judgment. But this stage is just a beginning, and it is certainly possible to use my intuitions as a heuristic device to move on toward more objective and descriptive techniques. For instance, I have been using Everett Shostrom's (1963) test of self-actualization or James Bugental's (1965) findings on self-actualization in "successful" therapeutic patients.

Science is really a division of labor and a collaboration. If I make value-statements, as I did concerning self-actualizing people, then my fellow scientists can proceed with less passion, personal involvement, and heat—in the cool manner of science—to check whether I was right or not and whether my intuitions were correct. Indeed, if only scientists with bright ideas and hypotheses existed, then we would have no science at all. We would have only a collection of bright ideas without any criteria for choosing among them.

Ninth, the Adolf Eichmann phenomenon is often raised against humanistic psychology's tenets. The question is usually phrased, "How about the Nazis who claimed that they were only doing their duty?" What shall I say about the particular value of obeying orders and being dutiful? Clearly, I must introduce the whole conception of the diminished human being. Indeed, this whole concept is vital to the coherence of the entire system of humanistic psychology.

I suppose that it may be necessary to accept the fact that the ultimate Being-values are those chosen not simply by "reasonably good" specimens but by the *best* specimens of the human species. Perhaps we can think of self-actualizing men and women as resembling the canaries in the old coal mines, who are far more sensitive than most of us about what is right and wrong, good and bad. This notion implies that our best individuals see the truth more clearly and that they can perceive the dim truth when others see only dark confusion.

This issue often has led to a discussion of the validity of illuminations in the peak-experience, that is, of *Being-knowledge.* I began to deal with this issue in the appendix of my book on the psychology of religion (see Maslow, 1964), but much more remains to be done. In any event, it must be admitted that, to an extent, I have proceeded on the assumption that this Being-knowledge is indeed valid in particular ways.

Tenth, I also feel, though I lack certainty, that self-actualization theory must confront the question of the superior person and his or her responsibility toward those mentally or physically inferior. How much should the self-actualizer become involved in seeking to help those who are diminished, either temporarily or irreversibly? Of course, our evaluations of others sometimes prove to be unreliable; for example, the drug rehabilitation program called Synanon has been very effective in treating supposedly "incurable" drug addicts.

Eleventh, it is important to emphasize that the term *good* applies only to the human species. It is quite possible that what we deem as good for members of our species would be bad for mosquitoes, bears, or tigers. The word is species-relative. Yet, intriguingly, ecological findings seem to demonstrate that the balance of nature is in certain ways good for all species simultaneously. The same phenomenon is clearly present among human families when there are conditions like abuse that are bad for everyone involved.

Finally, it must be stated that self-actualization is not enough. Personal salvation and what is good for the person alone cannot be really understood in isolation. Social psychology is, therefore, necessary. The good of other people must be invoked, as well as the good for oneself, even though it must be demonstrated how these are—or may be—synergic. To some extent, the individual's interests and those of his or her team or organization, culture, or society may be at odds—even though an overall principle of *synergy* may prevail. But, in any case, it is quite clear that a purely intrapsychic, individualistic psychology, without reference to other people and social conditions, is not adequate.

Certainly, these assumptions of self-actualization theory must be amplified into a more thorough formulation. But it seems worthwhile to specify some of these axioms that are not often enough made explicit when discussing human nature and its heights.

Throughout the 1950s and 1960s, Maslow steadily grappled with his influential concept of self-actualization. Well aware that all of his exemplars of self-actualizing men and women were living in Western civilization, Maslow was nevertheless sure that his concept would ultimately prove cross-culturally valid. In this brief, unpublished, and undated journal entry probably written in the mid- to late 1950s, Maslow offered forceful speculation about possible Eastern versus Western differences in personality growth toward self-actualization.

4

Can Monks Be Self-Actualizing?

Are inner-directed people of Eastern civilization such as Zen sages and Buddhist monks more emotionally integrated than self-actualizers in Western civilization? The answer may very well be yes, but the Eastern monks seem inwardly integrated at a much *lower* level of comprehensiveness than those who must integrate not only within themselves but also with a complicated, external world. To integrate inwardly and attain serenity at the cost of giving up the external world—in effect, escaping and avoiding it—is ultimately a form of phoniness.

Why? Because first of all, people in Eastern civilization such as Buddhist monks are self-integrating at the cost of other persons' *not* being able to do likewise. That is, Buddhist monks usually must be supported materially by others who are actively working in the world, and hence, such monks resort to endeavors like begging.

This situation reminds me a little bit of those who pseudomoralistically refuse to butcher meat but quite willingly eat the meat that *other* people butcher. Thus, supposedly spiritually-minded individuals who must beg to sustain themselves are not really contributing to other people and the world but rather seem to be taking from them.

To possess a mental "health" that is based on this kind of phoniness—and which is conditioned on the necessary "unhealth" of others—is ultimately as shaky as the ancient Greek democracy that was based on slavery. It is a situation like the brain-injured individual who avoids anxiety only by restricting and narrowing the world and having others provide full-time care. Or, it resembles the situation of the overprotected or overly sheltered child or the real but stultifying material security traditionally imposed on Mediterranean women. Or, it is like the seemingly rigorous cosmic philosophy of the 16th-century French philosopher Voltaire, whose confidently optimistic worldview collapsed after he learned of Lisbon's devastating earthquake.

In any case, the kind of selfish emotional-integration achieved by Eastern monks inevitably produces an inner dissociation or personality split. Of what real value is personal serenity bought only at the cost of minimizing, ignoring, or even denying the misery of others? One condition of true peace within is ensuring that peace of others.

This principle is relevant for all the *self*-ists in the realm of spirituality. One must take into account the dependence of the inner world on the outer world. It is a real challenge but a vitally necessary one.

The same principle pertains to monkish celibacy. Such a lifestyle provides an easy way to avoid the problems inherent in marriage and family life. To be sure, one definitely gains serenity by not having to assume any responsibility for other people. But such a life also means a "giving up" of the possibility for greater heights. In organized religion, celibacy seems essentially to be a safety device rather than a growth device, an avoidance of danger rather than an integration and mastery of it.

This whole line of analysis follows down the same slope of adjusting to the demands of the outer world via a lobotomy rather than adjusting to it by progressively widening one's mastery, growing stronger and stronger, and increasingly being able to take in the world. The latter approach is much more "mature" than adjusting to society's demands and responsibilities by avoiding problems.

Now, let us attempt to make this aforementioned principle balance with the equally valid truth that personal salvation cannot come solely from the world and from the outside. That is, the Buddhist claim that personal serenity is necessary for outer peace is just as valid as the Western claim that the latter is necessary to attain the former goal.

I'm reminded of the writer Carl Sandburg's[1] parable about the U.S. pioneers traveling west who wanted peaceful and cooperative neighbors. Going along the road, they met a group of travelers coming from the opposite direction and preparing to make camp. One pioneer explained to the incoming group, "We're leaving behind our former neighbors, who were all nasty and hostile. How are people in your community?" And one of the travelers answered, "Exactly the same." Then, another pioneer spoke up and said to someone else in the group making camp, "Well, our folks are leaving behind neighbors who were all kindly and caring. How are people in your community?" The reply: "Exactly the same."

The moral of Sandburg's parable seems to be that other people generally mirror our own personality. What do you do, then, in a place with a loveless atmosphere? The first thing is to make *yourself* loving, for you have helped to create the loveless atmosphere. Buddha once said to the world, "You are not the victims of an external law but of an internal cause."

This ancient principle certainly appears valid today. A hostile person living in utopia is still a hostile person and will even destroy it—unless it can change him or her first.

The big challenge, therefore, is for us to integrate the Western and Eastern conceptions of self-actualization and inner peace. The good world helps to permit the good person to *be* good. It also helps to create good children who are more likely to become good adults.

EDITOR'S NOTE

1. Maslow did not provide a reference for this material from Carl Sandburg.

During the socially quiescent years of the early to mid-1950s, Maslow increasingly turned his attention to the psychology of religion. Before conducting any empirical research on what he would later call peak-experiences, Maslow spent several years absorbing a great deal of material on comparative religion. Eventually, he became convinced that American psychology had badly overlooked the relevance of this field in developing a comprehensive view of human personality. In this brief, unpublished essay written in July 1954, Maslow set forth ideas generated by reading The First and Last Freedom *by Jiddu Krishnamurti (1954).*

5

Acceptance of the
Beloved in Being-Love

In reading the modern Hindu philosopher Jiddu Krishnamurti (1954), I think it is clear that to be *choicelessly* aware means to accept the experience—or the other person—as it is, without desiring to change or manipulate it.

To have this quality means to respect, enjoy, appreciate, and end-experience the other in a passive, accepting, and yielding way rather than in a domineering, interfering, "seeking," or even improving way. It is not possible to be completely immersed in a love-experience if we are simultaneously concerned with the end-experience, for instance, plotting a change here and a change there. Certainly during moments of great love, we do not compare this person with another—either physically or mentally. Rather, we experience the lover as an end in itself rather than as a means to an end. For all references and comparisons to other people at other places and in past and future time have the effect of undermining and limiting our experience. As such, they're completely irrelevant.

To be fully aware—as close to complete awareness as possible—means to focus wholly on the experience: to concentrate utterly, to pour one's whole self into it, and to be unaware of everything else in the entire world and in all of time. This state necessarily includes a nonawareness of one's own ego. Just as one knows that one has really listened to music because self-awareness disappeared (which also occurs during true creating and absorbed reading), so also is complete love marked by forgetting the self.

(Though limited as yet, the psychological experiments on problem-centering versus ego-centering are nevertheless useful in revealing that the act of forgetting one's ego is more possible for emotionally healthy people. Furthermore, that mental state also is more efficient for thinking, learning, and other activities.)

Yet, it seems to me that experiencing the beloved in *Being-love* is ultimately aesthetic. That is, I am defining aesthetic in this context as one's end-experiencing of *all* the sensuous qualities of the object, and this inner state significantly contrasts with abstracting, categorizing, and rubricating. The philosopher Filmer Stuart Northrop (1946/1979) offers the same viewpoint. In the long run, this same perspective is what Gordon Allport's ideographic-nomothetic distinction will in effect become. This notion too is precisely intimated by Krishnamurti's (1954) phrase "to be aware *of the present* without choice" (p. 41).

In other words, in the blissful state of Being-love, we truly experience the beloved "aesthetically." The appropriate words here are appreciating and enjoying. Of the two, appreciating seems more exact because it carries the proper connotation of passivity and noninterference. As Krishnamurti aptly comments, "How can there be a choice when you are confronted with a fact?" (p. 45).

Merely even to intrude ideals, standards, and theories of perfection serves to devitalize one's ecstatic experience and to take the blood out of it. We also learn this principle from psychotherapy, in which sheer, passive, free-floating listening without teaching, improving, demonstrating, or overtly helping turns out to be so curative and releasing. Indeed, this observation leads us to comment that "You can't really perceive the truth and be aware

of reality as it is unless you put aside all your hopes, ideals, and standards—
and just listen wholeheartedly." This situation encompasses objective and
true actualization.

Therefore, the thing to do is to let both things and people happen.

By the late 1950s, Maslow had become convinced that peak-experiences have many important implications for individual mental health. For example, he theorized that various forms of self-destructive behavior such as addictions might be cured therapeutically by inducing inner "peaks." In this unpublished article written in October 1960, Maslow offered his intriguing speculation about the health benefits of peak-experiences as well.

6

The Health Implications
of Peaks-to-Completion

Perhaps *peak-experiences* are essential for our physical well-being; that is, in some way, these are medically necessary for healthful living. If so, this fact might explain the prevalence of peak episodes within the general population, even though these may differ in levels of intensity. It seems possible that a person with great inner ambivalence and many warring, intrapsychic aspects could literally become insane from an inability to integrate peak-experiences.

The severely disturbed do not have peak-experiences; only the emotionally healthy do. In fact, the greater one's emotional well-being, the more likely one is to have peak-experiences. Likewise, the more peak-experiences we undergo, the greater our mental health becomes.

One reason why peak-experiences may be so vital to our emotional well-being is that they provide a climax, a complete catharsis and discharge. Conversely, the state of being unable to come to a climax produces a painful tension and probably creates toxins in the body. For example, think of the difference between the disorganized blood flow during inconclusive sexual petting versus experiencing a good orgasm. A total discharge thus seems necessary for our physical as well as our mental health. A completion ends striving and perseveration.

One could take up the whole question of the necessity for climaxes; for instance, compare the good ejaculation in males with the partial one. The Austrian-born psychiatrist Wilhelm Reich has discussed this issue in detail.

Without climaxes, how could a human being have rest and peace? Or real play of the *Being-value* sort? If not for climaxes and peaks that provide a sense of finishing, we always would feel in limbo—always striving and never satisfied—full of perseveration problems. We would also be *means* and never *ends*. Everything we did would feel like mountain climbing without ever reaching the top for a rest.

The truth is that any true gratification offers a small end-experience and permits nonstriving for a while. Sometimes, this end-experience can be acute and strong. But the really strong completions, the real states of finality—the real end-experiences beyond which there is nothing—the perfect climaxes: These are true peak-experiences.

In the full peak-experience, there are not only emotional aftereffects but also physical aftereffects. There is complete discharge—total depletion— and total satisfaction. A concrete example of this notion can be found in the male prostate gland, which discharges—either partially or fully. Chronically partial discharge of the prostate produces all kinds of medical problems leading up to surgery and probably even to cancer.

The full discharge is physically healthier too. Nothing is left to stagnate. Total discharge from this viewpoint must be qualitatively as well as quantitatively different from *almost* complete discharge.

The unused breast or the partially empty breast leads to pain, disease, and perhaps even cancer.

I suppose this situation must be the same for all the other ductal and ductless glands of the human body. The individual who is unable to experience a "good cry" after a calamitous event may suffer an eruption of skin blisters instead. It seems probable that the muscles themselves need total and violent contraction, if only for the sake of blood circulation, a real flow rather than stagnation.

This situation may relate to psychiatrist David Levy's research on atrophy during disease. For example, the unused intelligence tends to die. The partially satisfied love-need remains yearning forever. Real use must involve a total finishing discharge, gratification, and perfection. It seems plausible to make an isomorphism with a physical structure like the prostate gland and state that *no use at all means atrophy, partial use means abnormality, and only the full completion is healthy.*

It is true enough that the inability to complete an act varies from person to person. Some individuals are more impulsive in acting out than others. Some are more impatient or less capable of delay. But this reality does not alter the aforementioned principle. Every human being finds abeyance—that is, withholding expression—to be more or less troublesome or even intolerable.

Once more, the simplest physical experiences offer good illustrations of this notion. To urinate or defecate at the right time can be a great satisfaction, in the sense of culmination, total discharge, total emptying, and finishing.

In the psychic and social realm, we ought to become more aware of how much we live in the realm of continuing, perseverating incompleteness.

How many things are we disturbed about that we don't touch, fix up, or even discuss? How many indignant letters to the editor are never written? How many tempting tasks or ideas do we have to push aside forever, or at least delay, because we have other commitments already planned? How many "crooked pictures" are left hanging on walls that we're not permitted to touch? How much stupidity, inefficiency, or nastiness do we encounter that we must try to ignore? How much of our own indignation do we have to swallow?

We all have impulses to fix things, set them right, administer justice, and come to a final balancing of the books.

How many things can we do nothing about? How often do television programs, movies, or newspapers arouse in us impulses to improve the world, impulses that we can seemingly do nothing about? Certainly, this is one aspect that should be incorporated into the concept of modern alienation. That is, the industrial-bureaucratic world provides fewer opportunities for successful completions involving justice and the like. It allows us fewer experiences for fully satisfying our impulses for indignation, anger, or praise.

In essence, our public "books" thus remain perpetually unbalanced. But in our private lives, the peak-experience give us the vital sense of total completion.

✎ Drawn to music and art at an early age, Maslow always regarded aesthetics as a vital feature of human personality. For his master's thesis at the University of Wisconsin, Maslow had sought to study the psychology of music, but faculty rejected the innovative topic as inherently "unscientific." Though conducting in his later career little actual research on aesthetics, Maslow nevertheless viewed it as worthy of serious attention. He probably intended this brief piece, written in January 1950, as the foundation for a more comprehensive analysis.

7

Our Aesthetic Needs

Exploratory Notes

Very little is known empirically about our aesthetic pleasures, needs, impulses, creativeness, or, indeed, anything aesthetic at all. And yet, aesthetic experiences can be so poignant and aesthetic hunger can be so desperate that we are irresistibly tempted to postulate concepts that correspond to these subjective matters. It would be important to offer a theory to explain these acute experiences. There is only one thing we cannot do with our aesthetic impulses and that is to leave them alone!

It would be easily possible to scrape together out of common knowledge bits and scraps of evidence to support the postulation of aesthetic needs, just as we have done concerning the existence of cognitive needs. If nothing else, such bibliographic research would justify my theoretical effort and demonstrate the existence of an unsolved problem—a gap—a question that psychology today should attempt to answer.

Unfortunately, all we have to offer now—besides to cry "Problem! Problem!"—are a few distinctions suggested by other hypotheses to be discussed at a later date.

First, we must not think of *an* aesthetic need as if it were merely one particular impulse. Rather, there clearly seem to be discernible various kinds of aesthetic impulses, some or all of which also may serve as needs.

The aesthetic reaction is a subjective, introspective, and conscious response that most people consider ineffable; that is, it cannot be described in words but must be experienced to be known. However, some phrases are, in fact, used commonly to describe this type of experience. Thus, people frequently report such sensations as a faster heartbeat, a holding of the breath, feelings of fascination and mental absorption, sensations of sharp pleasure, and cold shivers moving up and down the back.

Indeed, I have often thought that the aesthetic experience may share a similarity with what physiologists call "sensory shock." For example, this encompasses a person's set of responses when suddenly immersed in ice-cold water. For now, I'm only guessing about this possible similarity, but at least it is easily testable.

The aesthetic experience may lead to various simple, habitual responses, such as collecting the particular objects (paintings, musical recordings, etc.) that give so much pleasure or going to art museums or musical concerts. In general, we may speak here of appreciation, fun, pleasure, and connoisseurship but not yet of *actual aesthetic creation!*

In both theory and practice, aesthetic creativity is separable from aesthetic connoisseurship and should be treated differently by psychologists. We needn't point only to the legendary violin virtuoso who hated music but also to the well-known fact that connoisseurs notable for their good taste are often not creative at all. Even in principle, the battle between critics and creative artists is endless.

In the realm of analyzing artistic creativity, an infinite number of distinctions and classifications seems possible. Most of these are of little use to psychology, and we shall not concern ourselves with them. However, there is one differentiation that is almost surely necessary, namely, that between expressive versus imitative inventiveness.

Expressive inventiveness needn't be communicative or social and is of considerable importance in the theory of psychotherapy. For example, a purely expressive painting may or may not have meaning for anyone other than its creator. Regardless of the painting's actual beauty, it may give its creator great pleasure and emotional release.

Avowedly communicative art is another thing altogether, for it may have any or all of the motivations that involve other kinds of communications—such as an academic lecture—and it may produce as many diverse kinds of effects. If our primary interest is aesthetic enjoyment and creation, then we are far less interested in communicative or purposive art than in expressive art. Sometimes a poem or a painting is as didactic as an academic lecture, or, perhaps, its purpose, while communicative, is yet aesthetic—for example, to depict or remind us of a beautiful portion of the world (to induce an aesthetic experience) or to create a decoration.

Quite apart from aesthetics, our intrinsic fascination with research about aesthetic impulses also may harbor theoretical importance. It begins to appear as if the aesthetic realm may be an important bridge to join psychology's field-theorists with those theorists who are interested in human needs or instincts.

The most primitive example of the aesthetic impulse is our desire to set wrong things right, in the interest of symmetry or of pleasing order or of composition. Aspects like incorrect proportions, clashing contrasts, and displeasing arrangements all seem to call out in us the impulse to rearrange, to improve, and to correct.

Of great theoretical importance is the possibility of attributing this situation either to our inner need or to the external disarrangement—or, perhaps more accurately, to the total situation that comprehends both forces as a single unit.

Undoubtedly, empirical research will be necessary to shed light on all these questions.

Maslow today is well credited for emphasizing the importance of self-expression and creativity as key aspects of the healthy personality. It is less well known that Maslow also emphasized that during our childhood, we all need strong external controls for guiding our proper inner development. Quite possibly, Maslow gained this perspective in studying informally during the 1930s with the Viennese psychiatric thinker Alfred Adler, who regarded the "pampering" of children as highly destructive to their emotional-social growth. This brief, unpublished essay that Maslow wrote in November 1957 offers a rare glimpse into his perspective on effective child rearing.

8

Limits, Controls, and the Safety Need in Children

Children, especially younger ones, essentially need, want, and desire external controls, decisiveness, discipline, and firmness. They seek firm limits in order to avoid the anxiety of being on their own and of being expected to be adultlike because they actually mistrust their own immature powers. Generally, children are unsure of their capacities for self-control and of their own ability to handle unfamiliar situations effectively. Without the presence of clear, external limits, children often become frightened, as if they're suddenly being asked to shoulder adult responsibilities. Their emotional state becomes akin to what therapists call *catastrophic anxiety*. Such a state also resembles the emotional condition that Anna Freud (1950) has termed *the fear of being overwhelmed by one's instincts.*

Part of our responsibility as adults is to control ourselves and our impulses adequately. Children cannot do this to a similar extent, and they know it. To ask them to accomplish this task without help, therefore, is to present them with an immense burden. Children typically react to such an adult expectation with fear—as though their parent has suddenly died and they are now being required to become head of the entire family.

For instance, closely observe a normal child in a frenzy of excitement and elation. Now, imagine if a neglected or habitually ignored youngster suddenly receives a great deal of adult attention, unexpected love, or intense caring. This seemingly fortunate situation may actually cause the child to become inwardly disorganized and disintegrated and to feel catastrophically anxious. The youngster may even lose all self-control and the ability to function integratively in mind and body.

Sometimes it is desirable to pick up such a child and hold him or her tightly until he or she calms down, that is, until he or she recovers self-organization and self-control, unity, and integration. (The German émigré neurologist Kurt Goldstein has written extensively on catastrophic anxiety.)

My thought is the individual's natural tendency toward unity, wholeness, and integration—and against splitting and dissociation—is the obverse of this situation. Thus, most people feel happier as they become more integrated inwardly and more frightened as they become less integrated, for we thereby lose our volition and its effectiveness. We lose our healthy ego, our "executive capacity." Our self-unity becomes disrupted.

All this pathology comes to pass (a) when children are presented with behavioral tasks that they are incapable of mastering or (b) when their adult protectors no longer allow them to be calmly and happily childlike but suddenly appear weak and expect the youngsters to make important decisions at home.

This psychological principle holds true even if children superficially may seem to *want* absolute freedom of impulses and seemingly *resent* external, adult controls. For example, we sometimes hear of young adults who bitterly and with hostility confront their indulgent parents by saying, "When I was a child, you should have *made* me do it!" Indeed, overindulged children often feel contempt, scorn, and disgust for their weak parents.

It seems appropriate to express this entire notion another way: Children need strong, firm, decisive, self-respecting, and autonomous parents—or else children become frightened. Youngsters need a world that is just, fair, orderly, and predictable. Only strong parents can supply these important qualities.

Though Maslow always had an optimistic view of human nature and its possibilities, he also saw himself as a realist. Thus, during the 1960s, he became increasingly impelled by the questions: "Why don't more people achieve their full potential in life?" and "What inwardly stands in their way?" In this unpublished article written in November 1966, Maslow offered a tentative but fascinating answer.

9

The Jonah Complex

Understanding Our Fear of Growth

Most humanistic and existential psychologists today believe that a universal aspect of human nature is the impulse to grow, to enhance and actualize oneself, and to be all that one is capable of becoming. If we regard this viewpoint as accurate, then it is obviously necessary to explain why most people don't grow to their full inner height—why they *don't* actualize themselves.

The model that I have found most useful in grappling with this problem is the old Freudian notion involving psychodynamics, that is, the dialectic between an impulse's existence and the defense against its actual expression. Thus, once we have accepted the postulate that there is a basic human impulse to grow toward health, full humanness, self-actualization, or perfection, then we face the necessity of analyzing all the blocks, defenses, evasions, and inhibitions that get in the way of the growth tendency.

For instance, it is useful to apply the Freudian terms of *fixation* and *regression*. We can certainly use the psychoanalytic findings of the past half-century to help us understand the fear of growth, its cessation, or even renunciation in favor of regression. However, I find that the Freudian concepts are insufficient in this domain. Therefore, several new concepts must be formulated.

As we take our stand on psychoanalytic knowledge and transcend Freud, we inevitably make the discovery of what I've called the "healthy unconscious." To state it very simply, not only do we repress our dangerous, distasteful, or threatening impulses, we often repress our best and noblest impulses.

For instance, in our society, there is a widespread taboo on tenderness. People often are ashamed of being altruistic, compassionate, kind, and loving and certainly of being noble or saintlike. Most obviously, this fleeing from one's own best nature is manifested among adolescent males. They tend to renounce ferociously all attributes that might conceivably be called feminine, sissy, weak, or soft in order to appear completely tough, fearless, and cool.

But this phenomenon is hardly limited to teenage males. Unfortunately, it is pervasive in our society. Often the highly intelligent person is ambivalent about her intelligence. Sometimes, she may even deny it altogether in an effort to be like the common or "average" person—in an effort, so to speak, to flee her fate as did the biblical Jonah. It frequently takes half a lifetime for the creatively talented individual to come to terms with one' own talent, to accept it fully, and to unleash oneself, that is, to be postambivalent about one's talent.

I have found something of the sort to be true for strong people: those who are natural leaders, bosses, or generals. They too get into a tangle about how to handle and regard themselves. The defenses against paranoia—or perhaps better said, against hubris or sinful pride—are all involved in such internal conflicts. On the one hand, the person has his normal tendency for open and joyful self-expression, for actualizing his best tendencies. Yet, he finds himself frequently in situations in which he must camouflage these very same capacities.

In our society, the superior individual generally learns to put on a chameleon-like cloak of false modesty or humility. Or at the very least, she has learned not to say openly what she thinks of herself and her high capacities. It is just not permitted in our society for a very intelligent individual to say,

"I am an extremely intelligent person." In our society, such an attitude offends. It is called boasting and generally arouses counterreactions, hostility, and even attack.

Thus, a statement of one's superiority—even though it is justified, realistic, and proven—is frequently experienced by others as an assertion of the speaker's dominance and a concomitant demand for the listener's subordination. It is hardly surprising, then, that the listener will reject such a statement and become aggressive. Such a phenomenon seems common to many cultures around the globe. Accordingly, the superior individual derogates herself in order to avoid counterattack from others.

Yet, the problem confronts us all. We all must feel strong enough or self-loving enough to be creative, to achieve our goals, or to fulfill our potentialities. As a result, the superior athlete, dancer, musician, or scientist is forced into a conflict between his normal, intrapsychic tendency to grow to his fullest height and the socially acquired recognition that other people are apt to regard his true stature as a threat to their own self-esteem.

The individual whom we call neurotic may be said to be one so impressed with the possibility of punishment—so afraid of counterhostility—that, in effect, she gives up her highest capacities, her right to grow to her fullest height. In order to avoid punishment, she becomes humble, ingratiating, appeasing, or even masochistic. In short, due to fear of punishment for being superior, she becomes inferior and throws away some of her capacity; that is, she voluntarily diminishes her possibilities of humanness. For the sake of safety and security, she cripples and stunts herself.

Yet, one's deepest nature cannot be altogether denied. If it does not show itself in a direct, spontaneous, uninhibited, and unleashed form, it must inevitably express itself in a concealed, covert, ambiguous, and even sneaky form. At the very least, one's lost capacities will express themselves in troubling dreams, unsettling free associations, strange slips of the tongue, or inexplicable emotions. For such a person, life becomes a continuous struggle, a conflict of the kind with which psychoanalysis has familiarized us.

If the neurotic person has strongly renounced his growth potentialities and self-actualization, then he typically seems "good," humble, modest, obedient, shy, timid, and even self-effacing. In its most dramatic form, this renunciation and its harmful consequences can be seen in the dissociated personality—the "multiple personality"—in which the denied, repressed, and suppressed possibilities finally break out in a dissociated form of another personality.

In all such cases of which I know, the presenting personality before split was of a totally conventional, obedient, passive, modest individual who asked nothing for herself, that is, who couldn't really enjoy herself and be selfish in a biological way. In such instances, the new personality that dramatically emerges is generally more selfish, fun-loving, immaturely impulsive, and less able to delay gratification.

What most superior people do, therefore, is to make a compromise with the wider society. They reach out toward their goals and advance toward self-actualization. They seek to express and enjoy their special talents and abilities. But they also mask such tendencies with a thin veneer of apparent modesty and humility or, at the very least, silence.

This model will help us to understand the neurotic person in another way, mainly as one who is simultaneously reaching out for his birthright of full humanness, wanting to grow toward self-actualization and full being, yet who, constrained by fear, will disguise or hide his normal impulses and contaminate them with a mixture of guilt with which he soothes his fear and appeases others.

To say it even more simply, neurosis can be seen as containing the same impulse of growth and expression that all animals and plants share but with a mixture of fear. Therefore, growth will take place in a crooked, tortuous, or joyless way. One may thus be said to be "evading one's growth," as the psychologist Angyal (1965) aptly observed.

If we concede that the core self is at least partially biological in the sense of anatomy, constitution, physiology, temperament, and preferred, biologically driven behaviors, then it also may be said that one is evading one's biological fate or destiny. Or, I could even say that such a person is evading her vocation, mission, and calling.

That is, she is evading the task for which her peculiarly idiosyncratic constitution fits her, the task for which she was born, so to speak. She is evading her destiny.

That is why the historian Frank Manuel has called this phenomenon the *Jonah complex.* As we remember, the biblical tale of Jonah was that he was called by God to prophesy, but he was afraid of the task. He tried to run away from it. But no matter where Jonah ran, he could find no hiding place. Finally, he understood that he had to accept his fate. He had to do what he was called to do.

In this sense, we each are called to a particular task for which our nature fits us. To run away from it, fear it, become half-hearted, or ambivalent about it are all "neurotic" reactions in the classic sense. They can be considered illnesses, in the sense of breeding anxiety and inhibitions, producing classic neurotic and even psychosomatic symptoms of all kinds, and generating costly and crippling defenses.

Yet, from another perspective, it is possible to see these very same mechanisms as instances of our drive toward health, self-actualization, and full humanness. The difference between the diminished individual, wistfully yearning toward full humanness but never quite daring to make it, versus the unleashed individual, growing well toward her destiny, is simply the difference between fear and courage.

Neurosis may be said to be the process of actualizing oneself under the aegis of fear and anxiety. It thus may be considered the same healthy and universal process but hindered, blocked, and shackled. Such a neurotic person can certainly be seen as moving toward self-actualization, even though he limps rather than runs and zigzags rather than moves directly forward.

10

The Psychology of Tragedy

I have been reading Maud Bodkin's (1934) book *Archetypal Patterns in Poetry* and find it extremely stimulating. Her general theme, running throughout the work, is that tragedy ultimately involves the conflict between archetypal dominance versus subordination tendencies within the individual—especially the hero—and also between the individual and destiny, nature, or God. The following, specific types of tragedy can all be identified and amplified:

1. The dethronement of the King or the Father.
2. Disillusionment—inevitable in growing up. It involves a child's loss of innocence, being ejected from the Garden of Eden.

    a. Any descent from high to low—that is, from power to weakness
    b. The climax followed by decline
    c. From the mountain peak into the valley, down toward death finally

    d. From triumph to ashes

    e. After gratification comes satisfaction and then boredom

    f. After strength comes coasting, fatigue, weakness, self-protection

    g. After the happiness of novelty comes satiation, familiarization, and boredom

    h. The fall of the King, the lord, the dominant one, the "golden boy," the "darling of life"

    i. From happiness down to inevitable unhappiness (it can't last)

    j. From innocence down to inevitable grim knowledge (which means from happiness to depression)

    k. The inevitable fall of the hero or prophet who is now seated on his throne

    l. From despair up to victory and then back down to despair

    m. From nothing up to something and then back down to nothing

    n. From consummation down to emptiness (such as hunger)

    o. Up to orgasm and down to sexlessness, being "spent"

    p. From orgy to hangover

    q. From youth down to old age

3. Ambivalence—Oedipal or any other. No perfection resolution is possible; that is, either gratification or frustration (it makes no difference which) leads to tragedy. A weakening or strengthening (either arm of ambivalence) equals tragedy. This involves the domination/subordination ambivalence in men and women.

4. The wrong choice to which one is then committed forever.

5. The existential conflict within the individual of the beastly versus the saintly. Unlimited versus limitations. Imagination versus reality. Nobility versus the ludicrous, the small, and the ignoble. It is important to observe that all existential conflicts are insoluble.

6. The life-altering "accident" (Thomas Hardy's novels). What would have been . . . We can imagine the mistake undone. "If only I had or hadn't . . ."

7. The closure of *Being-justice:* completion of the act, leading to the just but unhappy ending.

8. The lack of fulfillment, the cutting-off of growth: the early death; the crippling of the dancer, runner, or athlete; or the interruption of the smooth working-out of one's promise, faith, calling, mission, or vocation by external catastrophe, illness, or death.

9. The demand for exclusive love: unsatisfiable yet imaginable.

10. Release from tension and conflict never succeeds for long. It always comes back. Regarding death and rebirth, we may be ambivalent about rebirth and prefer to stay quiet and dead.

11. Regret over what cannot be undone. Remorse of any kind.

12. We glimpse paradise and know that we must soon leave it, *always*. Or, we may not be able to attain it again. Or, death has taken it away from us forever. This notion applies to all *peak-experiences,* or virtually all, for while one is dwelling in heaven or the Garden of Eden, there is, in the midst of all the happiness, the quiet realization that the experience cannot last and must come to an end. This awareness is absolutely inevitable, and there is no way out.

13. The inevitability of death, or aging, of going downhill, *no matter what we do.* We are helpless, impotent, and weak before death—either our own or anyone else's. This reality puts the lie to all pretensions of being heroic, godlike, and so on.

14. To fall short of our own ideal or of the general human ideal: to discover that you are stupid, that you will *never* be the great pianist or writer, or that you must give up your youthful dreams and accept second-class status. This is often the tragic awareness of middle age: the recognition that you'll never be what you dreamed of as an adolescent.

15. Impotent regret. Wisdom found later in life cannot undo earlier mistakes. The remorse that follows on psychoanalytic insight into the past and before one has fully accepted the past. For example, the deceased person cannot be apologized to ever again. Clearly, we must then see our former selves as less worthy than we'd thought, but nothing can be done in the present.

16. Most of these dilemmas are gaps between what we are and what we could be or where we are and where we could be. Dominance, subordination. Why does tragedy seem to apply more to men than to women? Why are virtually all the tragic figures in Western literature and history men rather than women? Does this fact indicate that all tragedy necessarily involves the masculine struggling for dominance and against subordination? More than women, men want to be high while they are actually low. The lost erection. The not-yet attained adequacy of the young boy. Sexual and other kinds of impotence. Castration anxieties as discussed by Sigmund Freud.

17. Youth equals "transient splendor."

18. The regret before death, on the deathbed. The story of Ivan Illich. Death as the "final examination."

19. There is no rest for the weary. There is no end to human wanting and desiring. Gratification of any desire stills that desire for only a little while and then makes possible the emergence of another, higher desire.

20. You can see catastrophe coming and they can't. See Arthur Koestler's dream of crying out for help while being attacked and strangled in a roadside ditch, but no one seems to hear or do anything about it.

21. The beautiful fantasies that will almost surely not come to pass. The harem fantasy of all the young men. The Lochinvar fantasy of the young women.

TRAGEDY IN
NEW PSYCHOLOGICAL LIGHT

I also can think of the tragedy of the more intelligent, insightful, and discerning, for example, watching the events culminating in World War II inevitably happen and yelling like mad for people to wake up before it was too late but not being able to affect anybody or anything.

Or, today watching the population explosion in Latin America and having a sense of futility about not being able to help in any way—seeing the waste of giving foreign aid to a country that must always be Malthusian.

The sense of helplessness, of inevitable tragedy without being able to intervene, that one gets in watching Act I of a well-known Greek tragedy or reading a book of this sort in which the tragic ending is seen from the very beginning. There are many situations in life of this sort, for example, watching the adolescent head for catastrophe while refusing adult advice.,

In Bodkin's (1934) book, she describes Eve with all her lovely innocence in the Garden of Eden. Eve is unaware of what Satan means, but as readers and watchers, we know, and there is absolutely nothing we can do about it. The poet Milton comments, " 'There sounds the note of tragic pity for loveliness doomed, and unconscious as a flower is of danger' " (p. 165).

Then, Bodkin discusses the pathos of human destiny. This is the kind of feeling that many people experience at weddings, when the presumably innocent bride and groom are so blissful, knowing nothing in their happiness of the storms that inevitably loom ahead. The newlyweds believe that they will never quarrel, but we older ones know that they will. We know that their marriage one day may even break up altogether and so we feel like crying in an existential way.

This kind of situation frequently occurs as older people look on youth in their brashness, confidence, innocence, contempt of the old, and unwillingness to heed advice. They are *inevitably doomed* to repeat every mistake we have made in our own youthful days. There is nothing we can do about it. But at the same time, the young are beautiful, lovely, poignant, and touching in their doomed transience.

Bodkin (1934) relates an additional quote from Milton as Satan for a moment was touched by Eve's beauty and innocence: " 'That space the Evil One abstracted stood, from his own evil . . .' " (p. 167). This remark raises for me the whole question of *countervalues,* which are probably involved in any definitive consideration of tragedy, in the relation between the strong and the weak (dominance/subordination) or in the ultimate human, existential predicament.

Milton in *Paradise Lost* touches this conception very aptly when he says of Satan, "But the hot hell that always in him burns, though in mid Heaven, soon ended his delight, and tortures him more, the more he sees, of pleasure not for him ordained; then soon fierce hate he recollects."

This notion relates to the tragedy of perpetual desire that must be unfulfilled. There are many other situations paralleling this one, for instance, the old man who falls in love with a physically attractive little Lolita, the little girl whom he must never touch, or the tragedy of the middle-aged man or woman who is already homely and yet still strongly sexed and who will never be romantically sought after again in life. He or she must accept a state of perpetually unfulfilled desire. Another example is of the college student who learns that his or her IQ is too low to fulfill earlier fantasies and dreams of great success in life. Now, these must be given up.

Bodkin's (1934) crucial point is that, "Tragedy *always* carries with it the suggestion of some continuance or renewal of the strong life that plunges downward into darkness." She also states that, "*Tragedy* communicates in essentially religious exultation the sense of the profound values that do not erase with the death of the mortal creatures that partially embody them" (p. 215).

I agree with this notion. It might be better to say that tragedy is different from other life situations because it takes us out of the *Deficiency-realm* and into the *Being-realm.* That is, tragedy confronts us with the ultimate values, questions, and problems that we ordinarily forget about in everyday existence. With tragedy, we live on the highest plane. No matter what happens to the particular hero or incident, the *Being-values* themselves continue, for they are eternal and last forever. Furthermore, they are so obviously beautiful and desirable that any trouble, unhappiness, or even tragedy is worthwhile. The Being-values make it worthwhile. Therefore, there is always a certain sense of exultation in most of the powerful tragedies as well as sometimes a feeling of catharsis or purging.

In essence, I want to add what I might call the *exultation theory*—or the *Being-value theory*—to the old catharsis theories that have sought to explain the power of tragedy on the human psyche. For I believe that the key issue is the sense of being called to great, important, and eternal things, away from the mundane and trivial. In this way, tragedy can give us the same feeling of inner cleansing and inspiration as entering a gallery of fine art, seeing a very beautiful person, or hearing about a very inspiring action of some sort.

Bodkin (1934) goes on to say that, "In the earlier books, Satan appears as a Promethean figure. The theme of his heroic struggle and endurance against hopeless odds wakens in poet and reader the sense of his own state as against the odds of destiny" (p. 239).

There is doom here because of the hopeless odds, but there are also pride and exultation because a Prometheus—even though fighting against a far stronger figure—is not afraid and will not give up. He will fight to the end. Therefore, we can admire him and admire ourselves insofar as we are also Prometheus.

Bodkin continues on the same theme, "The sense of destiny irresistible, yet man's will unmastered" is the general point here. "This agony symbolizes the profound antimony of modern consciousness—the general unlimited irresistible will of universal destiny, and *the* defined individual will existing within this, and inexplicably capable of acting on it, even against it" (p. 239).

It seems important to note Bodkin's stress on the human will, on dominance, strength, and courage in the face of certain defeat. This stance is itself a triumph. In daily life in our society, all the onlookers become very admiring when some little fellow, for the sake of a principle, will get into a fight willingly and knowingly with a much bigger fellow. Perhaps this is precisely where a sense of tragedy arises: The display of will and courage is itself so beautiful and yet must be defeated. Here again is where the existentialist makes such a point about courage as a final plus in human nature, in the face of all the despair, gloom, and inevitable defeat that exists.

Bodkin argues that something new historically arose. All of the Greek dramas, as well as Dante, were tragic in the sense of presenting total human surrender and humility before destiny, fate, or the gods. All that Dante could offer people during the Middle Ages was humility. Then came Milton with his image of Satan as rebellious though impotent, who rejected humility as an acceptable answer and kept on being rebellious and willful forever. Later came the poet Shelley with his Prometheus, in which rebellion actually ended in victory and a kind of utopia. Thus, tragedy in the old Greek or medieval sense no longer existed, that is, in the sense of impotence before the will of destiny or the gods. So, whenever we see this feeling of impotence in modern humankind, it looks like weakness, for there is apparently no fight in such people.

However, there are many Prometheans still left who assert in a Promethean way the qualities of human dominance, the self, and the human will. In these people, there is greater optimism about human nature and the human condition. That is, they don't believe that destiny must inevitably triumph; they believe in their own capacity to fight fate and win. (See the model of the Seabees during World War II.) Human beings always have felt subordinate, but now they have the possibility in the naturalistic world of becoming dominant and bosslike, perhaps conquering nature and being on top. Of course, this stance is only for those who have no gods to be impotent before. These are the individuals who must look for the godlike in humanity itself.

Obviously, all this sums to the notion that tragedy is ultimately an issue of dominance, strength, will, autonomy, self-esteem, leadership, power, hubris, pride, and responsibility, as well as the psychological problems that such traits pose. Especially for men, there is a great deal known about these aspects of the psyche. For example, we must clearly distinguish the problems that arise from *within the individual* from those that arise *within the external world.* The internal problems of pride, strength, dominance, and so on are those of the defenses against paranoia, grandiosity, megalomania, and the loss of sensibility and humility. Also, there exists the internal problem of the leader involving feelings of loneliness and the lack of personal confidants.

The external problems typically involve human jealousy and resentment toward the dominant one. Also, there is the important issue that people who are out of power feel enfeebled and desexualized by the dominant. Externally, the leader must worry that the attainment of power involves a loss of personal safety; that is, if you stick your neck out by assuming leadership, you are definitely exposing yourself to all sorts of dangers.

However, various psychological and biological factors are probably involved as well. Certainly, some people seem to need or want power and strive for it just for its own sake or because they are aggressive. But to complete the whole picture and perhaps deepen our conception of tragedy, the following analysis seems important: We already know that wise, fine, and self-actualizing persons *don't* seek power for its own sake. Power means nothing to them, they derive no pleasure from it, and so, they are apt to avoid it. This fact is true so long as there is no necessity for them to assume power. But when such a call comes due to an emergency or highly pressing situation, the self-actualizing person may accept it from a sense of personal duty, while knowing full well the pains and troubles involved in leadership. One feels suitable for the mission because Being-justice demands it.

This situation itself constitutes another kind of tragedy. The general Cincinnatus wanted nothing more than to stay at home on his beloved farm, yet he was called on to be the leader in the Grecian war. All he wanted was a peaceful life, but tragically, he couldn't have it. The same situation seems to have held true for later historical figures such as Thomas Jefferson or Charles de Gaulle and, as a matter of fact, for the most recent presidents of the United States, such as Franklin D. Roosevelt, Truman, and Eisenhower. It could be said that not one of them really wanted to be president. They were all decent people who were uninterested in exerting power for its own sake. They ran for political office after their first terms because they felt needed by the country or because they felt able to do a better job than other candidates.

Whatever the actual truth regarding each of these politicians, they can serve as examples to illustrate my point that people may seek power even though they don't enjoy it and would be quite happy to relinquish it to someone equally competent, capable, intelligent, or wise who was willing to take over. The same principle was true for Abraham Lincoln in his second presidential term, and it also must be true for many others who, with a sigh of disgust, will give up their peace and quiet and then pick up the reins of power in order to do the job better.

Another kind of tragedy with which we are more familiar now than ever historically is that of the individual who evades his or her calling, mission, or task. Because they avoid assuming power to do the job well, such persons necessarily develop *Being-guilt* and loss of self-respect. Certainly, the very fine person cannot evade his or her duties and tasks. Rather, the only way of acceptingly doing so is to find someone equally competent to do the job.

The English writer Colin Wilson (1959) has aptly addressed this point in his important book *The Stature of Man*. Wilson writes in a more sophisticated way than the general students of tragedy in literature who yet remain unaware that something new has appeared philosophically in our time. They are still speaking of the dethroned king, of defying or fighting the gods, of reversals of fortune, and the like. But contemporary tragedy is of a different order altogether.

Today, more than ever before in human history, we make our own destiny. Humanists have no deity on which to lean, no Olympian gods of the Athenian sort, no fate, no destiny, nothing supernatural, and nothing superhuman. They have no one to lean on but human nature itself. Of course, tragedies can exist in such a new situation, but these are of a very different kind than Bodkin (1934) describes in her evocative book.

Finally, it is important to emphasize again that all tragedies have been written by men and about men. As such, they are virtually all male projections of internal masculine problems, conflicts, and fears—that is, of becoming too big, of rivaling the father, of failing to gain the mother's approval, or of being punished in the Oedipal sense (i.e., of being ridiculed by the mother figure for being too weak, puny, and limp). Or, we can additionally mention the young man's traditional fear that the tribe's elders will punish him for becoming too brash and assertive.

I also believe that Nietzsche and his superman concept would be useful in this discussion. For Nietzsche, God was dead. Therefore, all the old-fashioned tragedies that depended on a god, or gods, had lost all their meaning. But, of course, there could be many new kinds of tragedies. For example, the contemporary notion of Taoistic receptivity seems relevant, as today there is an active science involving engineering and technology—with an underlying arrogance and blind self-confidence—that can make for tragedy of the old style. This would encompass the theme of human dominance being overthrown, confidence being wrecked, and arrogance being punished.

Finally, Bodkin (1934) mentions (p. 281) the essential and *Being-psychological* sense of tragedy or tragic mystery that seems adherent in the very core of human nature or the human condition. This sense comes from our godlike element and arises whenever we are forced to feel the wonder and awe of humanity's godlike apprehension—our "thoughts that wander through eternity" (p. 281)—yet simultaneously feel our ultimate powerlessness. It would be useful to look through my files on existentialism and the human predicament to research this theme. It involves the basic conflict within every human being—which is nonexistent in any other species on earth—that is between our aspirations, dreams, and hopes and our creatural, limited, and conditioned nature.

When Maslow became famous in the 1960s as a leader of humanistic psychology, he frequently found himself criticized for being too optimistic—even a Pollyanna—about human nature and its potential. Maslow never accepted such criticism as valid and, indeed, viewed most self-proclaimed realists as egotistically frustrated, even embittered, former idealists. In this unpublished article written in October 1967, Maslow offered an explicit, personal statement about this issue.

11

Yea and Nay

On Being an Optimistic Realist

I do not accept the general tendency in our fashionable intellectual world of literary criticism, art and music criticism, and political commentary. The general tone in this world of public writers and talkers is to stress helplessness, anguish, weakness, and powerlessness. Their typical message is that no one can affect the world, the government, other people, or even the self. There are some individuals who are exceptions to my statement, but they are few compared to the general tendency to be pessimistic, anguished, whining, and self-pitying.

I must confess that I just do not feel this way. I don't feel helpless, manipulated, or hopeless. I feel myself to be my own boss. I feel active and

EDITOR'S NOTE: This chapter was originally printed in the Association for Humanistic Education and Development (AHEAD) newsletter. Reprinted with permission.

self-directing. I have some say in determining my fate. As I look back over my life, I always have.

For instance, I recently wrote a protest letter to my two U.S. senators concerning the military takeover in Greece. If my letter does not in itself change our foreign policy, I don't give up or declare, "It's no use," "Nobody listens to me," or "I've wasted my time." I have not wasted my time, I would feel. I have done what one person among over 200 million people can do.

Why should I expect to determine American foreign policy all by myself? Why should I expect a couple of letters to affect the whole hierarchy of government? Am I the only person in the world? In the United States? Wouldn't such disillusionment and disappointment over the lack of response to my letters imply that I would want to be a dictator? To determine foreign policy all by myself? To have my own way? How about other people and their opinions?

I feel very democratic and realistic about this matter. There are many other people involved, and they certainly have different opinions. I think it is eminently compatible with human dignity—indeed, necessary for my dignity—that I clearly have my say. But it is not necessary for my personal dignity that everybody agrees with me immediately or falls into place as soon as I give the word.

I accept fully the democratic principle of being a "good loser" and a "good sport" about a political decision made democratically. If I am outvoted, my way is to assume good will and honest intentions (until the evidence contradicts this view), to swallow my disappointment or anger, and to shake hands and say, "the voice of the people has spoken."

And then I will keep on trying to make my voice heard or my arguments accepted. This is also a course within the democratic procedure.

In another context, many people experience shock, disillusionment, and hopelessness on learning that a trusted friend has behaved in a bad way. But this is the same kind of mistake—even a childish one—of demanding omnipotence, omniscience, and, in this case, even an X-ray eye.

I have learned to take for granted that many people with whom I am close, who charm me at first sight, or who look very noble to me will slowly go downhill in my opinion as I get to know them better and watch them behave in a wide variety of situations. (Fortunately, this is not always true. Often enough, the more intimate and lengthy the relationship, the more I respect or love that person.)

Shall I became disillusioned if somebody with whom I casually chatted in our first meeting is subsequently revealed to be surprisingly foolish, inefficient, or malicious so I that I become less charmed and respectful? Why should I expect to be a wizard or an all-seeing eye? Why should I expect to make infallible and unchangeable judgments on the basis of a brief conversation? Of course, one does not get to know a person well in a first contact. For my part, I would keep in mind that first impressions are often less likely to be better than tenth impressions because people, understandably, generally seem to make a favorable impression on first meeting.

In short, I do not seek perfection in human nature. To do so is a big mistake and a sure path toward disillusionment and unhappiness in life.

Perhaps Maslow is best known for his optimistic belief in individual achievement and fulfillment in life. Alongside such founders of humanistic psychology as Rollo May and Carl Rogers, Maslow emphasized the uniqueness of each person's contributions to the world. Yet, Maslow became increasingly sensitive in the late 1960s to the growing evidence for biological influences on human development. In this unpublished essay written in July 1969, he attempted to reconcile his psychological optimism with the seeming reality of biological determinism.

12

Biological Injustice and Free Will

It is important to take up the various questions related to individual capability and achievement. Essentially, it is a matter of accepting the reality of biological injustice and unfairness: that some babies are born healthy and others unhealthy, some smart and others stupid, and some beautiful and others ugly. This is a matter of luck, gratuitous grace, fortune, or misfortune. It is not something that we can do anything about. It is determined. It is a limitation on free will.

Furthermore, it is a fundamentally different phenomenon from social injustice, for which we can always direct blame outward. For any social injustice done to me, I always have an alibi. I needn't be forced into the position of simply accepting the fact of my inferiority, ill health, stupidity, ugliness, or whatever the particular aspect might be. Social injustice is easier to accept psychologically than biological injustice, which is a blank wall about which nothing can be done.

The reality of biological injustice raises all sorts of profound philosophical questions that focus on the issue of *deserving.* Do I deserve a good heart when I am born? Should I get credit for being born into a rich country like the United States rather than a poor one like Albania? Was it any of my doing, and can I pride myself on the fact that the country in which I was born has a large amount of coal, iron, and other natural resources? In no sense can it accurately be stated that I "deserved" this good fortune (or, as in the case of Albania, my bad fortune).

Then the question immediately arises: How can I be proud and humble at the same time? Or, what do the words themselves mean against such a background of randomness? What do I have a right to be proud about, and in what sense? Can I be proud of my good luck? No, I must give full credit for my good fortune to fate, destiny, the luck of being born. I cannot take these aspects for my own credit because I did nothing to bring them about. In this sense, I must be humble. For I am lucky to be an American citizen rather than an Albanian. Therefore, I must be humble and modest about being born in the United States and not take credit for it, so to speak, not be "proud" of it, in the sense that I can boast about something I have personally accomplished, achieved, or brought about.

Another question then arises: Granted the fact that one may be born with good luck or bad luck, yet there remains a great deal of leeway for free will, responsibility, and becoming an active agent rather than a pawn in life. There is a lot of leeway for helping myself rather than giving up and sinking, for doing the best that I can rather than whining.

That is to say, free will starts immediately after birth. What I *do* with my genetic endowment and my body is definitely more important than merely the given of my biological inheritance. I had nothing do with its creation. But what I make of my genetic endowment, my body, and whatever was given to me is my responsibility. And *that,* in a different sense, is a matter about which I can feel pride, shame, or guilt.

In this context, pride, guilt, and shame make real sense, because of the reality of free will, responsibility, and choice—but self-choice, free choice. I had no choice about being born a male rather than a female, being born with strong rather than weak eyes, or with weak rather than strong ankles. But I did have a great deal to do with the use that I have made of my brain, through all my hard work, studying, life planning, and the like. In this sense, I can accept both the facts of biological justice and injustice, good luck and bad luck, and *also* of free will, personal responsibility, and of being an active agent rather than just letting myself drift into becoming a pawn. I am certainly not responsible for having strong lungs, but I am responsible for having made the best of them and not hurting them.

The possibility that my colleague Oliver Smith [not his real name] may have developed his leukemia by using LSD a great deal is something that constitutes an important difference between us. I wouldn't take a chance on dosing my body with unknown chemicals that might be destructive, and as a matter of fact, I have never done so. Certainly, this has been my choice and responsibility. In this sense, I have guarded what was given to me at birth. In a definite sense, it's as if I were the caretaker rather than the constructor or creator of my biological inheritance. I am the caretaker of my talents, capacities, and bodily organs and can do either well or badly with them.

In this context, words like *proud, humble, shame, guilt, deserving, responsible,* and *choice* actually make sense. So I must ask myself, Where are the places in my life in which I can make a choice? Conversely, where are the places in which I cannot do so, where a choice already has been made for me? What may I justifiably feel proud about? What ought I feel ashamed about? Again, the issue comes back to leading one's life as an autonomous, active, responsible agent—a prime mover—rather than as a pawn.

Another way of phrasing this entire line of reasoning is to say that fate, genetics, and biology indeed set limits for me—limits beyond which I can do nothing. But within those limits, I inhabit a realm in which I can accomplish either a great deal or very little. This is the realm of free will and self-choice and, therefore, of responsibility and justifiable guilt. Even if I am a paraplegic, if I have cancer—as in Aleksandr Solzhenitsyn's (1969) brilliant novel *Cancer Ward*—if I have weak organs, or if I am dying, I still inhabit a realm of free will. Even to the point of death itself, each person has free will, responsibility, and choice. In their personal reminiscences of concentration camp life under the Nazis, psychiatrists Bruno Bettelheim and Viktor Frankl have both vigorously affirmed this point. Even in a concentration camp, one can still do one's job well or badly. One can still be dignified or undignified. A person can still be all that one is capable of being or less than one is capable of being. Even at the edge of death, one can still be an active agent or a helpless, whining pawn.

In this sense, anyone who does any task well is doing just about as well as is conceivable. This is a generalization that applies to all human beings under all conditions, all circumstances, and at all moments of their lives. And, if they do their task *less* well than they could, they should justifiably feel guilty. This is what I mean by *intrinsic guilt,* for such persons have violated or betrayed their own higher nature.

Of course, one must make sure that the job is not only done well but also *worth doing in the first place.* For example, I recently spoke with a man who was a vice president of a tobacco company. He was stricken with intense guilt about his work and was in real psychological trouble. He genuinely felt guilty but, unfortunately, was not strong enough to give up his job.

Another way of phrasing this notion is to say that your first responsibility is to be yourself honestly and fully. This little formula condenses many other formulas as well as encompasses the concepts of self-actualization, inner growth, and the like. What it amounts to is the acceptance of reality, the principles of reality, and the acting upon of reality. So even if I am born a paraplegic, I can still be an agent rather than a pawn.

Beyond this first and most basic responsibility, there are others as well that involve self-choice and free will. These are not as utterly determined as my biological inheritance. For instance, I have responsibility for other people—certainly for my children—for any baby, or for anyone who is weak or sick. But even such responsibility must be integrated with the fact that a person's first responsibility is to be himself or herself. This fact means that one cannot be everything to everybody else. One cannot be everything even to one other person, except perhaps to a child. One cannot assume full responsibility for any other adult, which is to say that one must allow the person full responsibility to be himself or herself. Of course, this situation is impossible if I attempt—even unwittingly through being helpful, kind, or overprotecting—to intrude, interfere, and shape the other person. I must allow people their own responsibility.

This circle of responsibilities can grow larger and larger. I will call it the *Love Identification Circle* or the *Responsibility Identification Circle.* The further it extends out from me, the less responsibility I have, yet, to some extent, I have responsibility for every living human being; for all living creatures and, for that matter, for nonliving things; and for the cosmos itself (e.g., not to destroy it).

In this context, I also can relate my notes on psychological success. Certainly, this issue partly involves the same acceptance and accurate perception of what actually exists, that is, of the reality of one's own nature, abilities, and so on. I can speak here of the noble carpenter, the self-actualizing plumber. I can point out that there is a danger in adhering to a single pecking-order or a single, monolithic hierarchy of superiority and inferiority. *Anybody,* any person whatsoever, under any circumstances whatsoever, can be a psychological success—at least in the above sense, of doing the best that one can and doing fully what one can—to be himself or herself and to accept the reality of himself or herself.

This principle holds true even at the edge of death, in the face of disease, and also in the face of one's own limitations. Solzhenitsyn's (1969) book *Cancer Ward* offers an excellent example on this point. He depicts how all sorts of people accept with courage and strength their disease, whereas others show timidity and weakness in response to the identical fate. Perhaps it might even be said that the great, profound differences that exist among people in conducting themselves as agents or pawns can best be seen in the face of such tragedy or during moments of great pain or trouble.

One might say that *the individual does not have to be victorious to be accepted by the gods.* This statement makes the point very well about psychological success. It also intimates that there isn't a single, monolithic hierarchy of success or failure in life but that many hierarchies exist. Perhaps ultimately each human being is a hierarchy onto himself or herself, because in the final analysis, one's task is to be oneself well. And of course, there is no rival in the whole world for this task.

Not only can any single person be victorious in this task of being himself or herself, but precisely in this sense, every person in the world can be victorious as well. Victory or success in life should not be defined in terms of someone else's defeat. This point must be stressed. I also must indicate that there are so many different kinds of quality, so many kinds of capacity, and so many jobs to be done that virtually anyone can be very good, even in the ordinary, social sense, that is, successful in hundreds or thousands of different ways. Therefore, we all can be proud of our accomplishments and become autonomous and self-actualizing.

It is a real danger here to want to outdo one's siblings, to seek to be victorious over them, or to be rivalrous or competitive in the sense of the zero-sum game (in which my winning necessarily must be your losing). Psychological success is a non-zero-sum game because everybody can win. Rather than seeking to defeat someone else, it is better to seek excellence and perfection in one's own accomplishments.

Another cogent way of phrasing the above notion is to think of psychology as what psychologist Joost Abraham Meerloo[1] has called "the science of free choice within the framework of one's personal and social limitations." Such a perspective solves all sorts of paradoxes involving free will and determinism—of accepting one's fate and yet being an active agent—of giving up one's alibis for biological injustice or bad luck and retaining one's underlying sense of self-esteem, self-movement, and self-choice.

Another worthwhile aphorism by Meerloo on psychological success and the agent-pawn dichotomy is the following: "As one among many, it is easy for the individual to feel impotent, but the world in which [we] move is made different by [our] presence there; [we are] responsible for that difference, not for the whole." This notion relates to the issue of how to integrate pride and humility, for example, how to be a self-respecting garbage collector or, equally, how to be a truly modest and humble king.

All of this discussion can be placed under the heading of individual self-esteem and the research that has been done to analyze it. It is important to speak of a healthy self-esteem and an unhealthy self-esteem. Also, I should mention the general finding that the lower one's self-esteem, the greater will be a person's loneliness, unhappiness, interpersonal incompetence, and the like. All of my own research on dominance behavior among both humans and lower animals fits in well here.

Finally, I think that all the writings on Stoic philosophy are quite relevant. It might be useful to reread the Stoic philosophers and look at their phrasings. Much of what I have been saying in this essay is simply the Stoic outlook in another format. As a matter of fact, much of psychiatrist Viktor Frankl's self-styled existential approach to human personality (see, e.g., Frankl, 1984) can be aptly called a form of Stoicism. This philosophical connection might be important to establish.

EDITOR'S NOTE

1. Maslow did not provide a reference for this material from Joost Abraham Meerloo.

By the late 1960s, Maslow was increasingly convinced that important individual differences in human personality functioning were due to inborn, biological factors. Specifically, Maslow came to speculate that self-actualizing men and women—those whom he sometimes termed "fully human" and who, for instance, often have peak-experiences—are innately predisposed to emotional health and societal achievement. That is, they constitute a very real "biological elite." With the growing strength of biological psychiatry today, certainly this subject has gained increasing salience. In this brief, unpublished article written on March 28, 1968, Maslow explored some of the troubling sociopolitical ramifications of this issue.

13

Humanistic Biology

Elitist Implications of the Concept of "Full-Humanness"

The conception of "full-humanness" is a quantitative one. That is, this notion implies that some people are more "human" than others. Concerning individuals such as psychopaths, the implication is also that humanness itself is altogether lost. Certainly, the question then legitimately arises about the psychopath: Can this person, who certainly looks like a human being, still be considered one—because he or she has lost some of the defining characteristics, sine que non, of human beings? For such a person has no conscience, no shame, no guilt, and no ability to identify with other human beings, that is, to really know or even care how they feel.

This sort of question inescapably leads us to the edge of a conceptual problem pertaining to a biological elite or aristocracy, or what one might even call a *biologically,* rather than socially, *privileged class.*

What will eventually happen with this political "hot potato," I don't know. I have not even dared to publish my theories or my exploratory data about the topic for fear of their being misused by others. I am afraid that if I raise the problem of the survival of the fittest simply for the sake of discussing it, clarifying my own conceptual outlook and testing it on a sound research basis, then many nonscientists will seize on the issue for their own selfish purposes. Indeed, this situation is exactly what happened in the post-Darwin era of the late 19th century. Many individuals used such scientific speculation to rationalize *economic* privilege, that is, inherited financial privilege that had nothing necessarily to do with the biological quality of the persons involved.

The problem of the "biological elite" has inescapably confronted me in my efforts to build a theory of the good society (*eupsychian* theory). For I have anticipated that when there is no longer social injustice to serve as an alibi or an excuse for one's own biological inadequacies, then there might well be a great increase of Nietzschean *ressentiment* or malicious envy of those who are more successful in their achievements.

Therefore, I have been wondering how to protect the biologically gifted from the almost inevitable malice of the biologically nongifted. The latter could claim with perfect reason that nature was unfair and unjust in parceling out good brains to some and poor brains to others. The only way I can see out of this dilemma in any future, one-world civilization is for the biological superiors (*alphas* or *aggridants*) to become a kind of priestly class to which is given less monetary reward and fewer privileges or luxuries than the average members of the overall population. The picture I have here is of the leaders of civilization—the sages, teachers, pioneers, and creators—composing something like the Grey Eminence figures of the past, like monks clad in the simplest garments and perhaps vowing to lead selfless lives of poverty.

Psychologically, there is quite an adequate basis for considering this vision as enabling us to set feasible policy. People who are fully evolved tend to take as their greatest rewards the *metagratifications,* that is, the *B-values* or *intrinsic values.* Such men and women are most happy when they are advancing beauty, excellence, justice, or truth. In a very real sense, these individuals can be paid off in such values rather than in terms of money, tangible objects, or sensory luxuries.

Even today, the issue of the possible existence of a biological elite is crucial for philosophically oriented biologists, because again and again the questions arise: Who is to judge how to evolve ourselves, which type of individual should be favored and selected, or who is to live and to die? Who is to decide the sex of our offspring, whether they shall be 7 feet tall, or the like? Will the decision makers be a federal commission, a global board, or a special group of physicians, biologists, or other scientists?

In effect, these questions are so large and complex and, as of today, so uncertain in possible answer that we can only feel inadequate to the task. My hope is that our sense of inadequacy will spur us onward to become aware of our complete unpreparedness for facing such decisions and then to help us to forge ahead and become more prepared than we are.

I have no doubt that there will be in emergency confrontations a tendency for some portion of the population to turn to the age-old, supposed sources of superhuman wisdom, like the Bible or a supernatural God (of course, spoken for by some earthly establishment). Certainly, most scientists believe that nobody is available to make these decisions except we humans ourselves. The question of how to select the most adequate and wise, the best people to make these awe-full decisions must, therefore, be considered an urgent program.

With enough supportive data to be at least plausible, I maintain that there are spiritual values or laws—or principles of choice—that not only motivate the best of humanity but also can serve as values for everyone: principles to guide us in these great choice-points that will face us very soon. Clearly, such a claim must be weighed and checked, examined and replicated, and tested very, very carefully again and again (see Maslow, 1967).

Perhaps it may turn out to be one way of avoiding, or at least blunting, the edge of the big question about a biological elite to phrase the matter in the following terms: How shall we constitute a board or commission of sages to help humankind make its choices about how to evolve itself, toward which ideal type of human to move, and how to biologically select the good and wise? This phrasing of the question may be less offensive or frightening than simply to state that some people are biologically superior to others.

And then, of course, all of these questions are already tied in side by side, simultaneously and isomorphically, with the really big question: How do we move forward toward the good society? What is the good society?

Throughout Abraham Maslow's life, he deemed it important that emotionally healthy people find ways to maintain and heighten their inner growth in the everyday world. Maslow never accepted the view that a monkish life was necessary in order to become an achieving and self-fulfilled person. In this unpublished article written during the mid-1960s, Maslow offered a variety of methods for better experiencing the unitive life.

14

Living in the World of Higher Values

The key question facing many emotionally healthy people today is, "How can I live in the *Deficiency-realm* (as I must)—that is, the workday world with its falsehood, fears, ignorance, pains, ugliness, sickness, and evil—and yet not forget the *Being-realm* and *Being-values,* including pure beauty, goodness, and truth?" Two excellent books that summarize classical religious, contemplative, and mystical techniques are Pitirim Sorokin's (1954) *Forms and Techniques of Altruistic and Spiritual Growth* and Aldous Huxley's (1964) *The Perennial Philosophy.*

Inspired by these and other works, the following are my own suggestions:

1. Sample things.
2. Keep your eye on the ends, not only on the means.
3. Keep to the end-quality of means.
4. Transform means into ends.
5. Fight familiarization. Seek fresh experiences.

6. Solve the Deficiency-problem (i.e., don't always regard the Deficiency-realm as prepotent over the Being-realm).

7. Attain higher consciousness (i.e., enriched, widened experience) and then permit it to become preconscious.

8. Cultivate periods of quiet, meditation, "getting out of the world," and getting out of your usual locality, immediate concerns, apprehensions, and forebodings. Periodically get away from time-and-space concerns, away from clocks, calendars, responsibilities, demands from the world, duties, and other people.

9. Go into the dreamy state. Slip into primary process thinking: poetical, metaphorical, out of the world.

10. Be law-abiding in a Taoistic way: concerning the laws of nature, reality, and human nature. Perceive the eternal, intrinsic laws of the cosmos. To accept or even love these laws is Taoistic and the essence of a good citizen of the universe.

11. Embrace your past.

12. Embrace your guilt rather than running from it.

13. Be compassionate with yourself. Be understanding, accepting, forgiving, and perhaps even loving about your foibles as expressions of human nature. Enjoy and smile at yourself.

14. Can you smile in retrospect at your own 5-year-old childishness, as you can at your own, present 5-year-old grandchild?

15. The Deficiency-realm is prepotent over the Being-realm and its precondition. You must avoid dichotomizing them. They are (or should be) hierarchically integrated. An either/or choice is not necessary. The firmest foundation for the Being-realm is to have satisfied *Deficiency-needs* (such as for safety, belongingness, or esteem).

16. Ask yourself: How would this situation look to a child? To the innocent? To a very old person who is beyond personal ambition and competition?

17. Try to recover the sense of the miraculous about life. For example, a baby is a miracle. Think, for that baby now, "anything could happen" and "the sky is the limit."

18. Cultivate the sense of infinite possibility. The sense of admiration, awe, respect, and wonder. It is possible to experience these emotions in the presence of the "good" person, hero, and saint.

19. The process of getting out of the world is facilitated by quiet, by no busyness or noise, and by no activity, distraction, or responsibility. Outer voices are usually louder than inner ones, and lower voices are ordinarily prepotent over higher ones.

20. To better appreciate your own present life situation, do not compare yourself with those seemingly luckier than you but, rather, with others less fortunate than you.

21. Engage in deliberate, experimental philanthropy. If sometimes you are no good for yourself (depressed, anxious), at least you can be good for someone else. Offer yourself philanthropically: your time, money, and services to help other people, such as children. Work for good causes. Give at least 1% of your income to causes with which you can identify and that help you to feel virtuous.

22. If you find yourself becoming egoistic, arrogant, conceited, or puffed up, think of mortality. Or, think of other arrogant and conceited people and see how they look. Do you want to look like that? Do you want to take yourself that seriously? To be that unhumorous?

ENTERING THE REALM OF HONESTY

1. Avoid letting yourself become accustomed or indifferent to seeing corruption, degradation, hypocrisy, immorality, and prostitution. In the most horrible example of dehumanization, some Jews in the Dachau concentration camp found themselves even becoming accustomed to the daily sight of persons being burned alive.

2. You must keep on smelling the stink of dishonesty. (You may have to bow your head, but you needn't like it!) You must keep your palate fresh (much bread and fruit today is no longer tasty). Retain an innocent eye and tongue. Act with innocence.

3. A gray lie is still a lie. You do not have to politely agree with it. You mustn't be ashamed to be good in a cynical world.

4. Never underestimate the power of a single individual to affect the world. Remember, one candle in a cave lights everything.

5. Remember, it took one child in the fairy tale to see that, "The Emperor has no clothes!" and then *everyone* saw it.

GENUINE DIGNITY AND PRIDE

How much of your dignity and pride depend on concealment and secrecy? How would you feel if people could always read your mind and know what you were thinking all the time? Or, if they could physically see you at all times—naked, without privacy or concealment, in all your private and secret activities? The dignity and pride that would then remain are your only *real* dignity and pride.

In order to regain authentic dignity and pride, try not concealing, not relying on external signs of validation (uniforms, medals, a cap and gown, labels, social roles). Show yourself as ultimately naked and self-revealing. Show your secret scars, shames, and guilts. Do not let anyone force roles on you. That is, do not act the way other people think that a doctor, minister, or teacher *should* act if it is not natural for you. Do not conceal your ignorance. Admit it.

REACHING THE BEING-REALM

1. Get out of the *Deficiency-world* by deliberately going into the Being-realm. Seek out art galleries, libraries, museums, beautiful or grand trees, and the mountains or seashore.

2. Contemplate people who are admirable, beautiful, lovable, or respectworthy.

3. Step out into "clean air" on Mount Olympus. Step into the world of pure philosophy, pure mathematics, or pure science.

4. Try narrowed-down absorption or close-up fascination with the small world, for instance, the ant hill, insects on the ground. Closely inspect flowers or blades of grass, grains of sand, or the earth. Watch intently without interfering.

5. Use the artist's or photographer's trick of seeing the object in itself. For instance, frame it and thereby cut it away from its surroundings, away from your preconceptions, expectations, and theories of how it *should* look. Enlarge the object. Or, squint at it so you see only general outlines. Or, gaze at it from unexpected angles, such as upside down. Look at the object reflected in a mirror. Put it in unexpected backgrounds, in out-of-the-ordinary juxtapositions, or through unusual color filters. Gaze at it for a very long time. Gaze while free associating or daydreaming.

6. Be with babies or children for a long period of time. They are closer to the Being-realm. Sometimes, you can experience the Being-realm in the presence of animals like kittens, puppies, monkeys, or apes.

7. Contemplate your life from the historian's viewpoint—100 or even 1,000 years in the future.

8. Contemplate your life from the viewpoint of a nonhuman species, for example, as it might appear to ants.

9. Imagine that you have only one year left to live.

10. Contemplate your daily life as though being seen from a great distance, such as from a remote village in Africa.

11. Look at a familiar person or situation as though viewing it for the very first time, freshly.

12. Look at the same person or situation as though viewing it for the very last time, for instance, that the individual is going to die before you see him or her again.

13. Contemplate the situation through the eyes of the great and wise sages: Socrates, Spinoza, or Voltaire.

14. Try addressing yourself, or talking or writing, not to the people immediately around you but over their shoulders, that is, to history's great figures like Beethoven, William James, Immanuel Kant, Socrates, or Alfred Whitehead.

Toward the end of Maslow's career, he came to regard the ability to feel— and express—gratitude as an important, badly ignored aspect of emotional health. Conversely, Maslow viewed the widespread presence of ingratitude in our society—whether among family members, neighbors, coworkers, clients, and caregivers—as a definite sign of emotional pathology. In approximately 1969–1970, Maslow wrote but never published this brief article. However, he incorporated its intriguing ideas into several of his last experiential seminars.

15

Regaining Our Sense of Gratitude

The quality of gratitude is important for emotional health. Both to prevent possible devaluing of daily life and to help retrigger *peak-experiences,* it is vital that people "count their blessings": to appreciate what they possess without having to undergo its actual loss. I have been developing several experiential techniques for accomplishing this goal.

One method is to imagine that someone you care about might die—or *will* die—soon. Think as vividly as you can how you would feel, what you would truly lose, and about what you would be sorry. Would you have any regret or remorse? How would you conduct an effective good-bye to avoid later feeling a sense of gnawing incompleteness? And, how would you best preserve your fullest memory of this person?

In this context, I would like to share a personal example. Before my ailing Aunt Pearl died of a chronic illness, I had sense enough to try pleasing her by offering a special gift: serving for a whole day as her personal chauffeur.

I felt good about this. In a direct way, it was an expression of my gratitude toward her. It was a good ending.

It was also a much more satisfying ending than what I experienced with the psychiatrist Alfred Adler, with whom I had a slight, inconsequential quarrel the last time we met before he suddenly died. As a result of this unsatisfying ending, I have felt a sense of incompleteness, repetitive rumination, and regret for more than 30 years. I wish that I had resolved the silly quarrel while Adler was still living.

Another technique for regaining our sense of gratitude is to imagine *oneself* to be dying—or to be on the edge of execution (the novelist Arthur Koestler [1960] discussed this state of heightened awareness in his autobiography). Then, imagine how vivid and precious everything and everyone looks. Imagine vividly saying good-bye to each of the persons you love best. What would you say to each one? What would you do? How would you feel?

These kinds of exercises can enable us to feel and express gratitude more easily. In this way, we will be better able to view our life from a higher, more satisfying perspective.

PART II

Re-Visioning Psychology

During Maslow's final months, he became increasingly convinced that humanistic psychology needed to be more precise in articulating its position. In his view, too many well-meaning advocates were glibly offering conceptually muddled declarations about the "inherent goodness of human nature." In the long run, he felt, such a situation only detracted from the movement's importance in counseling, psychotherapy, management, organizational development, and other realms. In this unpublished essay written in March 1970, scant weeks before Maslow's sudden death, he summarized several axioms about the human psyche.

16

What Is the
Essence of Human Nature?

For all of humanistic psychology, organizational development, and training-group culture, the same unwritten assumptions and articles of faith seem to exist concerning human nature. Yet, these are rarely stated overtly or clearly. It, therefore, seems important now to make these assumptions explicit:

1. As its basic tenet, the new image of the human psyche states that each of us has a higher nature and that this higher nature composes a basic part of our essence. Operationally, this notion means that under good conditions, people can be expected to manifest such desirable traits as affection, altruism, friendliness, generosity, honesty, kindness, and trust.

2. In addition to revealing all of the above-mentioned characteristics of *self-actualization,* the more highly developed person displays *particularly* a greater efficiency of perception, truth-seeing, and reality-seeing. This means that such persons are not only happier but cognitively more capable and in better contact with reality. (I am hereby implying that neurosis is not only an emotional but also a perceptual disorder, a type of blindness.) Besides showing greater efficiency of perception, such individuals also display a greater efficiency of behavior, that is, fewer emotional inhibitions, blockages, paralyses, and reductions of human capacity.

We could generalize this entire perspective by saying that the fully evolved person—the one whose higher nature manifests because of good environmental conditions—tends to be better at everything. This simply means that by any operational definition, such individuals tend to be better human beings.

3. We can define "good environmental conditions" primarily as comprising all those natural, social, and physiological aspects that foster self-actualization. In turn, such aspects also help toward *basic-need* gratification, because such gratification composes the primary path for higher evolvement and humanness and greater self-actualization.

4. A key statement is that human beings, if having lived under good environmental conditions in the past and also doing so at present, can be "good"—that is, what has generally been called ethical, moral, and virtuous. This viewpoint firmly rejects the various doctrines that postulate original sin or the basic depravity or evilness of the human psyche. This viewpoint also rejects any theory suggesting that human beings cannot be good or virtuous.

However, this perspective does not reject the various theories that state that human beings are sometimes good and sometimes evil. Why? Because such a statement is indeed true. That is, my stance does not claim that people are basically good, for such a conclusion is factually incorrect. In effect, my viewpoint claims that human nature can be good under certain conditions and then goes on to specify those conditions.

5. This perspective offers the essence of a new image of the human psyche—and, importantly, also a new image of society. The social element is inescapably intertwined with the intrapsychic, because basic-need gratifications—which are necessary for growth in the individual's higher nature—must come from interpersonal relations, various subgroups, and the wider society. This situation means that the "good society" can be defined in terms of its ability to provide basic-need gratifications for its members. In turn,

this situation means defining the good society as *that which makes possible self-actualization for its members.*

Certainly, this new image of the human psyche is part of an emerging *zeitgeist,* philosophy, or general worldview. If this image is proven to be accurate—that is, if it is sufficiently verified empirically—then everything in human knowledge and in human life must necessarily change as well. Certainly, it is obvious that all social institutions must change and that every product of human activity must likewise change. I am including the natural sciences in making this bold statement, for they too are products of human scientists. I would similarly expect that our overriding theories of nature—such as in biology, chemistry, and even physics—will change as a result of this new image of the human psyche.

6. It should be noted that today what is called management Theory Y—to which I would add my Theory Z—makes these same affirmations, because it states that many, though not all, people will improve under Theory Y assumptions and conditions.

7. With this entire outlook, an additional and necessary assumption is that the human psyche is *not* infinitely good, or always good, or even basically good. It is good only under the external conditions already specified. Under "bad" environmental conditions, people are more likely to show both psychopathology and evil behavior.

Therefore, in any discussion of Theory Y, or what I have termed the *eupsychian network,* or of the new image of the human psyche, it is necessary to specify that human beings are indeed capable of evil and sickness.

A necessary, scientific task here is to identify the specific environmental conditions under which psychopathology and evil will emerge. Some of these conditions are rather easy to identify because they are simply the opposite of the conditions that allow our higher nature to emerge—that is, that allow us to be good.

8. It must be recognized that many people reject on many grounds this entire worldview. These persons can be identified as composing a culture of despair—or even malice—in which qualities like cynicism and skepticism predominate. Such individuals generally believe that human nature is either incapable of goodness or is basically evil, or that what appears to be good can be explained away by a more fundamental interpretation that argues for our basic evilness, pathology, or selfishness.

9. Within the culture of despair, adherents are united in their belief that the human psyche's surface is misleading or false. That is, because these

exponents are confronted with the seeming facts that good people exist, good social conditions exist, and social improvement occurs, these naysayers maintain their skepticism, cynicism, and despair by attempting to argue that these facts are only superficially true and that below the surface a "darker" and more negative reality exists. From this skeptical viewpoint, what appears to the naked eye is less "real" than what is hidden.

10. It is possible to understand this skepticism, at least in part, by reinterpreting the history of ideas as generally composing a process of debunking, down-leveling, or devaluing human nature and humankind. I can generalize further than Sigmund Freud's famous statement that Copernicus, Darwin, and Freud himself inflicted three great blows to humankind's narcissism. That is, I would additionally mention other figures who were essentially "debunkers"—people who rejected the surface of things or what was apparent to the naked eye and instead insisted on the reality of some deeper, more debunking, or evil explanation. For example, I would mention the names of Karl Marx and Max Weber.

Many contemporary existentialists make Descartes the great villain because he emphasized the separation of mind and body, but I do not think this is accurate. However, I would add the figure of Plato, for his notion of nonmaterial (platonic) ideas or essences implies that what we see with our naked eye is less real than something else which we don't see.

We could also suggest the notion that the entire history of ideas is actually a history of debunking human nature. For precisely this reason, each attempted synthesis has failed. Nationalism has failed. Technological science has failed. The emphasis on general affluence and prosperity has failed. Organized religion has failed. Marxian socialism has failed. Monarchy has failed. The search for the philosopher-king has failed. Nobility, aristocratic, or upper-class rule has failed. For that matter, pure democracy starting way back with the ancient Greeks and through most of history has failed. (I don't regard American democracy as a failure, but it certainly needs a great deal of improvement; of course, many people do consider it to be a failure—mistakenly, in my view.)

11. Finally, I would reject the testimony of history as a true indication of the human psyche. Rather, it is only the story of what the human psyche has been, what humankind has yet made of itself. Contemporary knowledge of the fully actualized person and of the good, small societies shows us that history can be viewed as a statistical abstraction. That is to say, we can go back through history looking for self-actualizing people—saints, sages, and

others—and actually find them. Then, we can state the following: By selectively interpreting history in this way—seeking the very best that people can become—there is definite empirical support for these basic above-stated notions in our new image of the human psyche.

However, as long as the whole mass of humankind is lumped together in one statistical aggregate, then history must be viewed as irrelevant to our consideration of what the human psyche can be under good environmental conditions. For it has been very rare historically that large groups of people have experienced good conditions. There have never been good conditions for any mass of humanity except for the most temporary and fleeting periods of time.

Maslow is perhaps best known for his persuasive theory of human motivation—developed in the mid-1940s—with its hierarchy of inborn needs, the fulfillment of which leads to self-actualization. In his last years, Maslow became additionally convinced that all people have higher needs traditionally overlooked by mainstream philosophy and psychology. In this unpublished lecture at the University of Maine in August 1966, Maslow shared his evolving ideas on this subject.

17

Higher Motivation
and the New Psychology

I changed my plans this morning. What I had initially wished to discuss is the new psychology—this *Third Force* separate from the behaviorist and Freudian movements and typically being called humanistic or existential psychology. I had originally decided to examine this new movement the way a historian might do so, especially in terms of its new image of the human psyche.

For there is a dramatic change occurring in this conception. Such a sweeping change in how human nature is viewed occurs quite rarely—perhaps, only once within a century or even within two or three centuries. Now, we are at the edge of a real change in our image of the human psyche, and this revolution is what I had initially sought to discuss. We have enough time here today to accomplish this matter. But then, as I drove along in the car with my colleagues, I decided to alter my plans and to present something with which I am currently struggling—partly because it harbors great interest for the fields of counseling and psychotherapy and partly because it involves a fleshing-out of our whole, new, humanistic, and transhumanistic conception of human beings.

I do not have any notes with me, yet I am willing to try. I also confess that I am a little shy and timorous with the topic. Then, it occurred to me that this shyness has been a characteristic feature of my own intellectual work: Whenever something new pops into my consciousness, I initially fight it. In the psychoanalytic sense, I experience resistance often involving just plain fear. I develop insomnia, cold chills, even poor digestion. Yet, I also feel a kind of pride, as though I am wrestling with someone strong. And slowly, it dawns on me that something is cooking intellectually inside. So by now, at the age of nearly 60, I know that if I begin to suffer from insomnia, digestive problems, glumness, and grimness, it is actually a good sign. My wife will aptly comment: "Something good is cooking, isn't it, Abe?"

I am just at the point of developing a new theory, and I'm not quite courageous enough to fully accept its implications. It almost frightens me. I am scared of what it may mean in overturning mainstream psychological notions, and it rouses a whole conflict of pride and humility, hubris and fear. Well, let me try it, and if my voice begins to quiver, you will understand why.

THE NATURE
OF HIGHER MOTIVATION

Innocently enough, I began my investigation by attempting to examine the motivations of self-actualizing people—that is, actual men and women who were no longer motivated by *basic needs* because their basic needs had already been satisfied. Many more such people exist than you might suspect. Certainly, they are not common, but if you go hunting, you will find them—those whose basic needs have been satisfied and who generally feel safe and secure rather than anxious in the world. In essence, they feel a sense of belonging, of being part of the human family and not outside of it. Their love and affective relationships are good. Deep down, they feel worthy of love and affection. They have friends and, if fortunate, someone to love intensely. Their self-esteem problems have been settled well enough so that they respect themselves. They are not drowned with inferiority feelings; they have a vital sense of self-worth.

With such people, what happens? Some of them—but crucially, not all— embrace the *Being-values.* That is, they feel loyalty to these values and personally identify with them. To talk statistically, I would estimate that such men and women constitute the psychologically healthiest 1% of the total adult population in the United States. In virtually all of these cases, these individuals have a clear sense of mission about their lives, that is, a meaningful vocation or *calling.* In a very real way, they are involved in work that they love; the word job simply doesn't fit their lifestyle.

I have found myself looking through the thesaurus for older words and meanings related to *vocation,* for example, to have a vocation in the priestly, rather than in the grim, money-driven, sense. All my self-actualizing subjects have had vocations in this priestly sense.

Now, the next step occurred when I realized that these vocations or callings were in themselves apparently rather ordinary. For instance, one of my subjects was a practicing psychiatrist and just loved the field of psychiatry. Another was a woman who simply adored being the "clan mother," that is, making a full-time vocation out of having many children, becoming close with her nephews and nieces, and so on. Another was a lawyer who was utterly devoted to the legal field. So, you might say that the category of occupation or activity itself wasn't at all the key variable: A person could be a self-actualizing lawyer or a real stinker of a lawyer.

Rather, what constituted the big difference for self-actualizing people was that their activity became a channel or medium for expressing the eternal, ultimate values—the true, the good, the beautiful, the just—in everyday life. For example, one man might become furious at injustice and then just roll up his sleeves, drop whatever he was doing, and work like mad, staying up late at night, in order to battle and defeat injustice. He would experience very profound satisfaction in bringing about justice.

In speaking to this man, I realized that he *loved* the law: He talked about it as one might extol a sweetheart. He even seemed willing to die for it. In the same way, another person might feel the same way about the value of artistic beauty like music and still another about uncovering truth through scientific discovery.

This realization astounded me. I remember rereading Plato's *Republic,* in which he stated that the ultimate good involves the contemplation of the ultimate values. What was so amazing was that I had found men and women in everyday life who were embracing, actually *living,* these ultimate values through their particular activities. They could be attorneys, educators, scientists, or grocery store owners, but in a real sense, they were sages or saints. Yet, they did not exude halos. They wore shirts, belts, and shoes like everyone else.

I confess that it took me a while to assimilate this observation. All my life, I had expected saintly or noble people—those who love justice or beauty— somehow to look different, more heavenly. To change my erroneous outlook, I developed all sorts of mental exercises, and I have shared these with my college students over the years. I now think that it is possible for me to look at a person and clearly state without corniness: "That man is a sage to the degree of 14%."

That is, I began to realize that *everyone* has at least some of these higher qualities. So, the major question is, "How much, to what extent does he or she possess saintliness?" And, "How scared is he or she of this saintliness? How much is he or she repressing it?"

So, I finally have reached a point of thinking: Everyone in this room has a certain degree of saintliness—in the sense of wisdom, of loving justice and being willing to fight for it, of being what is sometimes sneeringly called a "boy scout" or a "do-gooder." The best descriptive term I know is from the Jewish tradition involving the Hebrew language—a *Tzaddik*. It does not carry any pernicious or invidious connotation in our culture. A *Tzaddik* is one who combines the best features of the saint and the politician, one who embodies both wisdom and pragmatism.

In American culture today, most people are very reluctant to think of themselves in this way. They would much rather prefer to be seen as tough, hard, strong, and never tender-minded about anything. But I have learned to break through the barriers that people feel about their saintly qualities. I may say to a seemingly tough-minded businessman, "Now, look here. If anybody is doing something good, I'm going to assume he's a boy scout. So what are you a boy scout about? What good or beautiful things are you trying to bring about in the world?"

And people often blush when they hear such direct talk. They truly blush, and this is really the only way I know to get most persons to blush. To ask them about sex won't do it. But if I ask them to confide their highest motives and impulses, they probably will begin to blush. And if I pursue this line of questioning and "accuse" them of loving virtue, then they will often admit, "Yes, I would like to bring about such-and-such noble event."

IDENTIFYING WITH THE B-VALUES

My next step has been to consider that the Being-values, which such people had embraced in their lives, actually had become defining values for them. In other words, these values—beauty, justice, truth, and so on—had become in Freudian terms interiorized or introjected, taken into their own being and digested there. The Being-values had become part of the self, and if someone attempted to remove these values from such individuals, it was like ripping out a bodily organ. In a sense, such an action could be harmful, even lethal.

Then, I gained a further insight. If the Being-values exist both inside the person and outside, then exactly what is their essence or form? Something very peculiar arises for which we lack an appropriate vocabulary. For my basic identity—the very way in which I conceptualize my inner being—thereon includes something of the outer world. If the Being-value of truth becomes so important to me as a scientist that I cannot even conceive of living without it, then truth is out there, too. It is within you as equally as it is within me, and suddenly, a paradoxical unity has taken place. The seeming dichotomies between selfishness and altruism, self and others, and my being and everything else in the world have been transcended. I've taken the world into myself, so to speak. The world is in my own blood.

At this point, you can read all sorts of writings by Far Eastern philosophers and sages and Western thinkers like Spinoza, and things begin to make sense. Perhaps all of the world's major religions have offered metaphorical phrasing about the truth of this psychological situation. Now, of course, I am attempting to phrase my analysis as a scientist and not as a minister, priest, or rabbi.

And what I would like to accomplish next is to put my theoretical investigation to the test empirically and determine the following: To what extent is my hypothesis true that self-actualizing, healthy people have internalized the Being-values into their lives? If so, then how can we help move larger numbers of men and women to identify more fully with these values? It might make sense to begin our definition of the good human being by assuming the active presence of the Being-values and then providing specific methods for heightening these in everyone. Such an approach might be called *meta-counseling,* combining the roles of regular counselors, psychotherapists, and educators.

Suppose everything I have been saying turns out to be empirically true, that these Being-values are indeed the highest human motivations—those shared by the most psychologically mature, healthy, and evolved. As a *meta-counselor,* I could thereon say to a person, "These are the motivations that you'll graduate to if you've been lucky enough, if life has been good enough to you, and if you live in a good enough society so that you obtain all the love, respect, and esteem that you need. Once you feel sufficient self-esteem, self-worth, and self-respect, you'll move into another motivational domain."

I am calling it the realm of *metamotivation.* It exists beyond the hierarchy of basic needs. For the *Being-needs* certainly are not *Deficiency-needs* in the ordinary sense that a baby needs love, so that you just kiss it, snuggle with it, hug it, and kiss it some more until the baby is satiated. The psychiatrist David M. Levy called this technique *replacement therapy*—essentially, providing the tender, loving care that originally failed to take place.

Well, the Being-values obviously are not Deficiency-needs. They are *metaneeds,* and they have a different quality. What I am describing now is growth motivation, and *growth-needs* are quite different from Deficiency-needs. For one thing, you never get bored with growth. Never. This is in direct contrast to the basic needs, which can definitely become satiated.

For example, suppose you like eating a good steak. You may relish the first one and even enjoy eating a second, but eventually you know that too much steak will make you nauseous. The same thing is true for love—certainly for physical love and even for verbal expressions of love. There comes a point when you just do not want any more physical or verbal affection. You have enough.

But the same process does not occur for the Being-needs as motivators. There is never a point when you would say, "I don't want to hear truth anymore" or "I don't want to see any more justice."

And now, I have arrived at a totally new point in my theorizing. I admit that I am skating on thin ice empirically, but the ideas just won't let me sleep; I'm getting the old insomnia again. Somehow, I have come to the hypothesis that to be deprived of Being-needs leads to emotional illness, or what I am calling *metapathology.* If there are 16 different Being-needs, then 16 kinds of emotional illness or metapathologies exist.

For instance, I am suggesting that being consistently denied access to the truth in daily life will lead to definite emotional difficulties, and to be consistently denied access to beauty or to justice also will lead to definite inner problems. In a very real sense, I am arguing that every human being has an intrinsic need to experience the B-values in daily life and that deprivation or frustration of these needs will cause emotional problems.

Can I buttress my theory with any concrete examples? Yes, because human history has unfortunately produced entire societies—like Nazi Germany or the Soviet Union under Stalin—where the populace has been denied truth or justice, and all sorts of definite pathologies arose. Plenty of places exist on the globe today that lack a free press or where citizens don't dare say certain things in public for fear of being jailed or shot. Well, I am suggesting that certain kinds of emotional pathologies will arise in such societies. That is my point.

Less pernicious as a destroyer of B-values but nevertheless harmful is the impact of commercial television in American society. I believe that its influence is utterly immoral, corrupting, and damaging to the human spirit, especially to children who have so little ability to cope with its power. They watch a program with an impressive hero and then during the commercial break that same figure tells his youthful audience, "Okay, kids, now I want you to buy this breakfast cereal!" or "This is the toy that I want you to tell your parents to buy!" In this way, American television is undermining children's capacity to experience truth, and I am sure that this situation is leading to metapathologies among them.

Or, let's take the Being-value of beauty. What would it be like to live every day in a totally ugly world in which beauty no longer even existed? Well, we know something about this matter because we have plenty of ugly places around us—for example, hideous urban neighborhoods—and we can see what these do to the human spirit. Certainly, it causes some inner illnesses but not illnesses in the sense of the American Medical Association's current list. I am not talking about diseases that invade an otherwise intact and healthy human organism. Nor am I talking about some minor, easily remedied condition. Rather, the metapathologies are systemic diseases and, therefore, affect the individual's whole mind and body.

For example, let's consider a person who inhabits a society in which access to truth is denied; such an individual will develop a whole set of adverse emotional, and probably even physical, reactions to that way of life. Or, let's consider a youth who lives in an urban neighborhood totally lacking in beauty in which everything is brushed with ugliness. That condition will have significant emotional and probably even physical effects.

If you follow my line of reasoning so far, what I'm suggesting is that the Being-needs are necessary for our total health in daily living. It might well be that we need only small doses—the counterparts of our bodily needs for magnesium or zinc—but that these inner requirements are nevertheless real and inescapable. Just as we need to ingest a certain amount of magnesium or zinc in our diet for healthy functioning, I am suggesting that we all need to ingest or experience unadulterated truth, justice, or beauty for our inner well-being. The lack of these minerals or vitamins will inescapably cause certain kinds of illnesses, and I believe that the lack of the B-values will do likewise.

Now, do you see the enormous social implications of my viewpoint? If a baby is living in poverty with an inadequate diet, then any social worker today will immediately say, "Yes, that baby isn't getting enough B-vitamin complex in its diet at home. We have to supply it, or the baby's going to become ill." Well, in the same way, social workers, counselors, educators, and psychotherapists of the future will have to say, "That baby is growing up in a place without the B-value of beauty. We'll have to expose it to beauty to prevent a metapathology."

If you accept my argument, then you can see how I have moved the whole discussion of values, philosophy, and the like into the biological or physiological domain. It is no longer just a nice abstraction to say, "Human beings need to live in a just world" or "Human beings need to experience beauty in their lives." Rather, we are attempting to say that each of us is born with certain innate needs to experience higher values, just as we are born physiologically with the need for zinc or magnesium in our diet. So, this argument is definitely saying that our higher needs and motivations are biologically rooted.

I admit that this is a hard argument to accept. We are accustomed to believing that human nature is infinitely malleable and that people can become whatever their environment tells them to be like. But my data clearly suggest otherwise. Therefore, we have to start seeing ourselves in a different light. This is what I mean by saying, "For centuries, human nature has been sold short." For my theory is implying that in a certain sense, every newborn baby is a potential Plato. Every child has an instinctive need for the highest values of beauty, truth, justice, and so on.

If we can accept this notion, then the key question isn't "What fosters creativity? How was a Beethoven created?" But it is "Why in God's name isn't *everyone* a Beethoven?" That is what has to be explained now. Where was the human potential lost? How was it crippled? We have got to abandon that sense of amazement in the face of creativity, as if it was a miracle if anybody created anything.

To adopt this perspective is to become what I call the Taoistic helper who holds back from shaping, molding, and directing the individual. I am not saying that babies do not need our help in order to grow. Of course, they do or they will die. But we ought to be guided by a kind of American Taoism. This would mean that as parents, educators, vocational counselors, and so on, we consciously supply children with their Being-needs just as we deliberately give them vitamins to help meet their physiological needs for zinc, magnesium, or calcium. Nowadays, good parents don't say, "Well, maybe little Johnny by chance will get enough calcium to be healthy." Instead, they make certain that Johnny's diet contains an adequate amount of such minerals or vitamins. In the same way, parents of the future will say, "Johnny needs to experience beauty, truth, or justice while growing up. We have to supply these Being-needs or he will suffer."

This sort of approach is what I mean by metacounseling, guiding but not coercing the individual to experience the Being-values. Vocational counselors can have a tremendous role to play in this matter. I remember when I discovered psychology in college. I had been struggling with law, geology, and mathematics, and this was so different! It was like falling in love with someone. Ideally, one's vocation is an expression of the self: It is a way of finding one's identity, one's real self. The luckiest person in the world is the one who gets paid for being in love: who is fascinated by something and finds that he or she can make a living by it. From this perspective, an effective metacounselor will help people discover their own unique potentialities and do so in what I call a Taoistic, noninterfering way.

SUMMARIZING PRINCIPLES

For me now, there is sufficient evidence on this subject of higher motivation for it to be persuasive. I admit that it might not yet convince a rigorous, experimental psychologist. Most of the supporting evidence thus far is clinical and personological rather than laboratory-controlled experimentation, although I am fairly sure that such validation will eventually come. In some respects, it already has. Based on the available evidence, the following key principles can, therefore, be set forth:

1. Every human individual has a higher nature, far better than we have ever suspected. This realization is part of the revolution underway in psychology today, and it is gaining solid research proof, even from studies of our primate inheritance.

For instance, there are a lot of impressive, laboratory data showing that monkeys will perform all sorts of tasks simply to look out a window in their cage and see what is occurring in the room around them. Monkeys will work like mad to gain a few seconds just to peek out a window. You can see the hungry look in their eyes. Likewise, it has been found in the laboratory that monkeys prefer to look at moving rather than stationary things. With the increasingly sophisticated design of such laboratory studies, it is possible to study the preferences of monkeys or human babies for various activities, sensory experiences, and the like. So we already can say that all humans have an instinctive need for curiosity and that our motivation to experience novelty is innate.

2. Human beings can improve psychologically and *do* improve psychologically. There is a lot of argument now raging about this broad issue, but I are not saying that humans can become psychologically perfect. They cannot, except perhaps for a moment or two. Rather, I am only stating that humans can improve and, furthermore, that we should help them to do so. Psychotherapy and humanistic education should become the science of helping people to improve. Also, I am not implying that human progress is inevitable and infinite, as some thinkers believed at the start of the Enlightenment in the 18th century. Progress definitely will not happen automatically.

There is a lot of laboratory research evidence with lower animals like white rats to indicate that a stimulating environment is crucial for healthy organismic development. That is, without living in the appropriately stimulating environment, growing white rats experience brain atrophy. This empirically driven principle seems even more valid for humans.

3. Human society as a whole can improve. It can be improved, and it *does* improve. Again, I am not implying some notion of perfect progress, nor am I saying that any society can become perfect. Rather, I am merely suggesting that human society is improvable, that the task is up to us, and that we can learn how to accomplish this effectively. Be aware: To say this is not to deny that our species might blow itself up tomorrow in nuclear catastrophe. That is also possible. Societal improvement is not inevitable.

4. The fully functioning human being has a zest for life. Many youngsters today erroneously believe that good people are somehow boring, dull, and bland. A lot of neurotics enter psychotherapy insisting that they do not want to give up their neurosis for fear of becoming uninteresting. But that is not an accurate way of viewing personality growth; it is just another way that human nature has been sold short. Rather, to pursue the Being-values and to be virtuous and psychologically healthy are the most exciting things in the world. It is not boring, it is not bland, and it is not dishwatery.

5. All persons have a right to actualize their potential. In principle, any newborn baby in the world has the capacity to do so and can be helped to do so. This notion certainly would lead us into a whole discussion of the ideal human society and its obligations to each of its members. For example, what does equal opportunity mean in this context? In American society today, babies have terribly *unequal* opportunities for personality growth in terms of both the basic needs and the metaneeds. This situation must be changed.

6. All humans compose a single species. This statement seems quite clear. In principle, therefore, it would seem to make sense that we should be able to develop a one-world kind of politics.

7. Humanistic and existential psychologists are more aware than ever that all persons possess certain underlying needs and values and that if these are denied, denigrated, or unfulfilled, then certain forms of illness or meta-pathologies will result. Furthermore, it looks as if humanistic science—in the broad sense—can help to supply these crucial values for human beings. This viewpoint signals a tremendous revolution in scientific theory, which has always been defined as being value-free.

8. Finally, heaven exists within this empirical system. It is inside the person. It happens only occasionally, particularly during peak or mystical experiences, and it is typically transient and brief. This evidence suggests that we must change our belief about happiness as being a permanently attainable state of consciousness. Rather, my research indicates that people always seek higher and higher heavens, that the most glorious peak or mystical experience—with all its real happiness, joy, or ecstasy—does eventually fade and lose its novelty and impact. Whether we had a lifetime of 500 or even 1,000 years, it is human nature to seek new experiences.

From this perspective, we have to abandon our age-old conception of heaven as a state of blissful retirement. There is a great deal of clinical evidence now that if you love fishing or listening to Beethoven's music and decide to retire to enjoy these activities all the time, you are eventually going to become miserable. Yes, your happiness about experiencing such activities was real, but satiation nevertheless takes place. So in a sense, we have to prepare ourselves for the inevitable letdown after ecstasy and bliss and understand our desire for greater and greater heavens as basic to human nature.

Well, I have been doing an awful lot of talking this morning. It's all about my new thinking about metamotivation, the higher human motivations. I am convinced that such ideas will become increasingly important in the future development of humanistic and transhumanistic psychology.

Throughout Maslow's influential career, he argued that modern psychology had neglected many vital aspects of human personality. Among those he often cited were our emotional needs and capacities for altruism, aesthetics, creativity, completion, justice, love, and truth. In this unpublished lecture presented at a graduate seminar at Brandeis University in March 1961, Maslow offered his freewheeling thoughts on the paradoxical aspects of happiness and sadness, particularly as revealed through peak-experiences.

18

Laughter and Tears

Psychology's Missing Values

Aesthetic experience is missing from psychology. In larger terms, values are missing from the field as well. So far, truth is the only value to be emphasized, and even this one really is not regarded as an ultimate value. I would like to make a proper place for values in a general theory of human nature.

Let's start with humor. If we think of the world's finest people—those who are self-actualizing—we generally have a rather somber image. We conceive of such individuals as being very sober, even imperious. Interestingly, this outlook is also true for our conception of the Judeo-Christian God: never humorous but always stern.

Such a conceptualization itself raises a very intriguing question: Why don't we ever imagine great people as giggling? In any case, I report to you

99

that the self-actualizing persons whom I studied were not at all grim or humorless. Nor was their humor cathartic or hostile. On the whole, it embodied what I have termed *philosophical humor, educational humor, existential humor,* and *self-actualizing humor.* Of all the historical and contemporary personages whose lives I have studied, Abraham Lincoln seems to have most displayed this humor in a perfect way.

Where does such humor arise in the human psyche? Not merely from our sensations of pleasure or happiness or even from the *Being-realm* in general. We would be obliged to conceptualize bigger, fancier, and flossier words. We would have to talk of *ecstasy, rapture,* or *bliss* rather than mere pleasure. Also present is the element of sensing the cosmic absurdity, the intrinsic absurdity of the human being and of human relations. For example, I see the image of the lowly worm who is attempting to be a god or of the primate who is attempting to stand on his hind legs. There is a necessary mockery that we must make of our own pretensions. On one level, our pretensions are certainly serious, but on another level, they can never really be fulfilled. For ultimately, our pretensions rest on ignoring the reality of death.

In the experience of love and also of true aesthetics, laughter frequently arises. The novelist Thomas Wolfe has described this phenomenon very aptly: When we see something beautiful, we have a tendency to laugh in a kind of exultant way. Seemingly paradoxically, we also have a tendency to cry: A beautiful thing can be so damned beautiful that it can bring tears to our eyes.

THE UNITY OF PLEASURE AND PAIN

Are pleasure and pain related in the human psyche? Yes, I have observed that at the highest levels of our existence there is a resolution of normal dichotomies, including those pertaining to pleasure and pain. Certainly, for most people throughout history, these two qualities stand as polar opposites along a continuum. That is, the more pleasure in life, the less pain. Or, the more pain that one experiences, the less pleasure. But among the best, self-actualizing men and women, this apparent polarity is resolved, and the two qualities somehow become interwoven or fused together.

Many examples exist about this lofty inner state. In *peak-experiences,* pain and pleasure inherently are intermingled. The most obvious example of that is love. On the usual continuum of pleasure, we can list such situations as smoking a fine cigar; eating a delicious, gourmet meal; attending an engrossing play; and so on. But can love for another human being be placed along the same continuum? It doesn't appear so. It has a different quality entirely.

During the highest pleasures of lovemaking and sexual orgasm, people sometimes describe a kind of "beautiful pain" and, quite spontaneously, a sudden awareness of death. Here, in the most life-filled situation imaginable, death somehow walks in through the back door. Why? Perhaps because there is a certain inevitable sadness about finishing anything intensely fulfilling— whether it is in lovemaking, painting, or writing a book. Certainly among many authors, the emotional state of "postpublication depression" is quite typical. One feels sad and depleted. So, a kind of resolved dichotomy indeed exists. The seeming polarities of happiness and unhappiness, pain and pleasure can be transcended, and we must, therefore, speak of them in a different way. The facts about them become different.

For this reason, we can accurately say about love: the more pleasure, the more pain; the more happiness, the more sadness. We can gaze with an ecstatic feeling of love—with an exalted sense—at a child who is delightedly playing yet simultaneously feel a sense of sadness. For we know the disappointments, pains, and troubles in life that the child will inevitably suffer. We also know the inevitability of death.

I remember the day that my first daughter, Ann, got married. It was very nice and all that, but suddenly I burst out crying. I felt ashamed in front of the guests we had invited, but I had to express that emotion. Afterward, I tried to analyze my reaction. The wedding had been a peak-experience, and I had certainly felt very happy, as had Ann. Yet, in the very midst of that happiness, I had definitely thought, "Ann believes that life will always be like this, that she will now live 'happily ever after' with her husband." And when I sensed the inevitable letdowns and disappointments that life had in store for Ann, I couldn't help but cry.

So, in any experience of great happiness, there is also a concomitant aspect of sadness. Pleasure becomes embedded with pain. We gaze at a beautiful flower and feel sad because it will die in a day. It ends. We know that we won't experience it forever. We too must die one day.

During the state of *Being-cognition,* we perceive death as existing in the present moment. For instance, as you stand there before me, I see that you are physically deteriorating. You are not what you were 10 years ago. This awareness brings sadness to me. Right now, I can see the troubles you are going to have. For instance, you don't know as much as I do about the very real psychological difficulties of middle age. We all know that we are going to die, but we do not know what death is like. In the fullest perceptions of Being-cognition, an awareness of death is present. This is simply what has been reported to me by those who have had peak-experiences.

Keep in mind: I am not introspecting here. I began this topic with my subjective introspection, but these reports are provided consistently by many others. Admittedly, at first, such descriptions were startling to me. We are not used to thinking in such terms.

My theorizing in this domain specifically began with the sexual histories that I took in the mid- to late 1930s. My interviewees often recounted this sense of sadness, pain, and death during the moment of orgasm. The happier the moment during lovemaking, the greater the ensuing sadness. It was as if the two qualities were bound together closely. You love someone very much, and you look at her and realize that she is mortal.

In other words, I am redefining empirically our normative definition of happiness. I am reporting to you that the happiest, most ecstatic moment of bliss or rapture has within it an element of sadness and poignancy. In an odd way, this sadness is a beautiful thing. Should we take it away, we may destroy the peak-experience.

A related principle: Insight carries a sense of tragedy with it. For example, suppose at the age of 40 you discover that all your previous attitudes about life were wrong. Suppose you realized that essentially you had spent 20 years of adulthood in wasted, stupid battling. All that time is gone. It can never be regained. With this awareness, you cannot help but feel very sad.

Another example pertains to the fleetingness of the moment. Suppose you had one peak-experience in your life and then none ever again. This is a sad thing to undergo, for it means that you have been in heaven and been cast out. The modern English writer C. S. Lewis (1956) discussed this phenomenon in his book *Surprised by Joy*. He had undergone a peak-experience and consciously tried, unsuccessfully, to re-create it. He then felt an element of real tragedy and realized that we must be "surprised" by joy for it to exist.

Frequently, we feel almost a sense of regret after a peak-experience as we ask ourselves, "Why can't life be like this all the time?" Or, when we achieve a sudden insight and feel so wise, we often ask ourselves, "Why must we be so stupid? Why must humankind be so stupid?"

Imagine yourself on a kind of mountain peak with a curving, meandering river below. The people on the river are slowly journeying upward while others are coming down. They all are embedded in the momentary situation. They cannot see what lies ahead, but you can. That is, you can see both their past and their future. You can see what is occurring at the fork of the river or at their later place of arrival. But there on the mountain peak, you cannot change the river. Furthermore, I report to you that in the state of Being-cognition, you don't *want* to change it. You are a contemplator, an observer, a Taoist noninterferer. Or, imagine yourself as watching a play. Within the drama, the characters do not know what is actually happening, but the godlike spectator does.

During peak-experiences, you have a loftier perspective than those who are embedded in the situation. Therefore, you have a sense of sadness or of absurdity. It is as if you are sitting on a fence and watching two sides fighting a war and sadly saying to yourself, "This conflict is absurd." You can be sad and smile at the same time.

For instance, in thinking about human stupidity or mistakes from the immediate Deficiency-world, we can feel very negative about events like Nazism. But if we are observing from a much higher, 5,000-year perspective, then we can permit ourselves to understand the event rather as painfully foolish.

It is necessary for us to shift back and forth constantly between the Being-realm and the *Deficiency-realm.* For even if we are on that lofty mountain peak, we must return at least once in a while to the daily struggle below. A full psychology would bear in mind that while we are journeying on the river, we must be able to think of the mountaintop vision as well.

For instance, in one moment, I may be discussing in class exalted and noble subjects and later find myself engaged in a battle with the academic dean over a seemingly trivial, administrative matter. But both states of being are necessary. In a way, the struggle with the academic dean originates in the mountain-peak, visionary experience.

Attempting to see the Deficiency-realm from the perspective of the Being-realm is an important endeavor. Certainly, our everyday behavior will change if we attain the viewpoint of eternity. It is Dostoyevsky's Ivan Illich who never reaches the peak and who has a totally trivial, idiotic life.

If we cannot return to this Deficiency-world without carrying some of the eternal world's peak-values with us, then we are behaving stupidly, trivially, and foolishly. Furthermore, we can inwardly tear ourselves apart.

SENSING THE COSMIC ABSURDITY

Does the feeling of sadness also encompass humor? Humor is an emotional regression, but it is a healthful and desirable regression. Real sadness or tragedy in the classical Greek sense can definitely be seen as humorous. Certainly, we cannot take life absolutely seriously. Generally, too, people who can be humorous about seemingly sad events are more likable. It is a sign of their emotional strength, not weakness.

For example, I remember hearing that when my mother-in-law was dying of uric poisoning, she began to experience hallucinations. She saw little people walking around on the wallpaper, and then realizing that these were illusory, she joked about the hallucinations. In other words, she was able to see humor about her physical pain and trouble. I certainly feel that marriages would be stronger if husband and wife could make less of their individual illnesses.

Generally, women report that men are lousy patients: A minor cold becomes a huge cosmic tragedy. The women find themselves acting motherly toward their husbands and babying them. This is all right, but the men look absurd. I think we would have greater approval for people who could adopt a more eternal view of the whole matter and not become so totally caught up in the actual, painful moment itself.

Let's take an extreme situation. Do you know of the humor of the black poet Langston Hughes? Or of the essence of traditional Jewish humor? Such sources suggest that sometimes in the course of human life, the inability to laugh will literally kill you. You have to be able to see the absurdity in the whole situation, perhaps especially in the stupidity of your exploiters or oppressors. Langston Hughes has written about the sadly absurd situation of black people who live in the United States. He has suggested that if they can laugh at the insanity and ludicrousness of their oppression, then these folk may be psychologically better off.

I remember conversing once with psychiatrist Bruno Bettelheim about tragedy and comedy. He made a good point in suggesting that the emotional problems of American blacks will initially increase as they gain greater power and acceptance in wider society—that the self-contained security of the ghettos will vanish and inescapably lead to new forms of anxiety and stress. Many blacks with whom I speak seem to have an unrealistic belief that racial integration will solve all of our social problems. It is a simplistic belief akin to thinking that marriage automatically solves all problems and that newlyweds "live happily ever after." But nobody lives happily ever after in marriage. Hopefully, people will advance from focusing on stupid problems to more intelligent problems.

The real danger of theorizing about self-actualization is how we can integrate the mountaintop vision of heaven—in which past and future blissfully dissolve—with the Deficiency-world necessity for active engagement with social problems. Thus, civil rights workers can talk wonderfully about a future age of justice and harmony, but then they have to fight in order to be served a mundane cup of coffee. But this battling has to be done, and it is not trivial.

We must not adopt only the idealistic Eastern viewpoint of life; we also need the pragmatism of the West. If we are faced with real injustice, we can't say to ourselves, "Now, just lie down acceptingly before the butcher's knife, for it will all work out well in 3,000 years."

Self-actualizing people can live in both of these realms successfully. For instance, I knew the anthropologist Ruth Benedict well. She was a great human being. To some extent, Benedict was detached from the world. She was a poet and would exclude herself at least an hour each day from phone calls, professional meetings, and the like. She led a private, restricted life. Yet, Benedict was also quite actively engaged with helping to create a better world through her anthropological fieldwork, teaching, and writing.

What role does personal courage play in all this? I have found that it is easier for us to be courageous at the age of 40 or 50 then when we are younger. An eternal human problem seems to be how to integrate our high hopes and ideals with the sense of our own limitations or of human limitations in general. We may look like a hero to the rest of the world, but we know damned well that we are a limited animal.

How do we integrate our godlike qualities with our creaturely qualities? This is a fundamental problem, and if you in this class turn out to be fine adults, then you will have solved it successfully. You cannot become a fine psychologist unless you take your own past onto your shoulders. You have to develop a bit of grandiosity in your aspirations and goals. Otherwise, you are just a fool or a dilettante collecting seashells on the beach.

Yet grandiosity is a great danger because, of course, we are not gods. We sweat, and we die. Somehow, it is our task to put together both of these qualities. On the one hand, if we cannot manage our sense of fallibility, then we are going to become paranoid persons. On the other hand, if we cannot retain our heroic ideals, then we are going to be bad, nasty people. To develop too much unchecked grandiosity is to become a paranoid individual. To become too focused on our limitations is to become an obsessional.

In closing, always remember: Without humor, there is paranoia.

By the mid-1940s, Maslow's interests had shifted decisively toward human motivation and personality. He had just formulated his seminal concept of the "hierarchy of inborn needs" and was beginning to grapple with new theoretical issues about the essence of human nature. With an optimistic temperament, Maslow unequivocally rejected the gloomy Freudian perspective that self-gratification is the overriding human drive. Written in 1943, the following paper represented Maslow's unpublished lecture notes for his personality course at Brooklyn College.

19

Is Human Nature Basically Selfish?

OUTLINE OF POINTS

1. All value systems about human nature are rooted in psychological assumptions; that is, man is either *selfish* (evil, weak, stupid, foolish) or *unselfish* (good, kind, cooperative, intelligent, rational). Or else, the particular value system involves a combination of these two perspectives (such as a belief in aristocracy or divine monarchy or that "You have to frighten people into being good").

   As a corollary to the above viewpoint, each of the following figures can be seen to espouse a definite if tacit view of human nature: John Calvin, Jesus Christ, Sigmund Freud, Adolf Hitler, Thomas Hobbes, Alexander Hamilton, Thomas Jefferson, Martin Luther, Jean-Jacques Rousseau, Arthur Schopenhauer, and Adam Smith.

2. Throughout the centuries, one's view of human nature always has been a matter of faith, theology, or philosophy. But now, science has come onto the

scene so that we may feel full confidence that an ultimate, definitive answer will eventually be found. Even now, many elements of the scientific answer are available to us. At least *some* scientific analysis about human nature is possible today.

3. Semantic confusion surrounds the problem. Words like selfish and unselfish have no commonly agreed-on meaning. An analysis of unresolvable arguments usually reveals unconscious or hidden differences among definitions. These words simply are not suitable for scientific discourse. Even within the conversation of the same person, particular meanings can vary.

   By semantic trickery (the hidden definition), one can prove that either all people are selfish or that all people are unselfish.

4. The only completely selfish person known is the psychopathic personality (interpersonal psychopath). Yet, the psychopath can behave unselfishly. We must, therefore, differentiate among the selfish act, impulse, and person.

5. Are there any completely unselfish people? Discuss the following: the masochist, neurotic dependency, the slave, full love-identification. These examples show again the necessity for differentiating human behavior from motivation. A psychodynamic approach, therefore, is necessary. Pure behaviorism can ultimately breed only confusion. It also is necessary to distinguish between "healthy" and "unhealthy" motivations.

6. The argument from observation of animals. Pseudo-Darwinism. The chimpanzee species, closest to the human, shows unselfish behaviors such as cooperation, altruism, and love-identification. To argue about human nature on the basis of animal observation is logically invalid. But if someone else raises the argument, it can be countered by pointing out the evolutionary basis for unselfishness.

7. *Selfishness* correlates with emotional insecurity and *unselfishness* with emotional security, self-actualization, and psychological health in general. Thus, we can say that unselfishness tends to be a phenomenon of inner abundance, or relative basic gratification. Selfishness can be seen as a phenomenon of basic deprivation, inner poverty, and threat—past or present. In an issue of *Psychiatry,* Erich Fromm's (1939) article titled "Selfishness and Self-Love" raises worthwhile points in this context.

EXPLORATORY NOTES ON
SELFISHNESS AND UNSELFISHNESS

THE SEMANTICS OF SELFISHNESS

At the outset of this discussion, we can introduce a very large increment of clarity by highlighting various semantic considerations. Indeed, anyone already familiar with this conceptual field would expect such an introduction.

As usual with any problem that deals with basic and important aspects—especially if the problem is an age-old one—it almost certainly involves a confusion of words used in different ways by different people, arbitrary impersonal definitions, confusion of symbols with realities, and all sorts of illegitimate abstractions.

If the problem is pursued by day-to-day conversations with a particular person who adheres to either extreme viewpoint, one easily finds that ultimately the whole argument will rest on some implicit, unconsciously held definition of the words selfishness and unselfishness. It has been my discovery that people who are willing to say that all human beings are completely and normally healthfully selfish will ultimately accept the following definition of selfishness: *Any behavior will be called selfish if it brings any pleasure or benefit to the individual.*

But a little thought will indicate that this definition prejudges and presolves the whole problem, because it automatically views all or practically all of human behavior as functional, that is, designed to produce some sort of benefit or pleasure to the individual. Such an approach is an effort to prove the case by arguing from a hidden, preconceived definition.

What can be done to counter that viewpoint? Several approaches may be taken. For instance, we can quarrel with the definition by pointing out that, after all, differences exist in human behavior and that there is something that must be called truly unselfish behavior. Or else, we can accept the definition for argument's sake and go on from there to emphasize that it is still necessary to distinguish through words the actual, realistic differences of which any individual is aware in relation to his or her own behavior or that of others.

For example, if I treat a child cruelly on Monday and then kindly on Tuesday, certainly the child makes the differentiation between these two forms of my behavior. Even if we grant theoretically that all behavior is ultimately selfish, then we will still have to distinguish between "selfish-selfish" and "unselfish-selfish" behavior. After all, we cannot make real differences disappear by verbal tricks. We still must recognize that in actual, daily practice, human beings distinguish between what they—even if mistakenly—call selfish or unselfish.

Another way of saying this is the following: In the real world, we find differences in behavior, even though such differences may not be reflected in the conceptual world. But when such differences do exist in the real world, they also should be reflected in the conceptual world. For example, we have a right to insist on some differential labeling for the following kinds of behavior: offering food to a starving friend versus refusing to give food to the same starving friend. Certainly, it is inadequate to describe both forms of behavior as selfish. In short, to attempt to eliminate a problem by verbal means is no solution to that problem. It will still remain, and we will simply have to use other words.

It is also necessary to point out that the same issue holds for the admittedly smaller number of theorists who claim that all humans are essentially unselfish. They typically employ something like the following definition: *Any behavior that does some good or benefit or that brings pleasure to someone else is unselfish.* Such a statement automatically describes all human behavior as unselfish simply by a preconceived definition.

The semanticist would make another point, which is that value judgments are attached to the words selfish and unselfish. Certainly in our culture, the word selfish has negative and undesirable connotations. Conversely, the word unselfish usually has virtuous and desirable connotations. The semanticist knows that when values are attached to words, then trouble and confusion are sure to result.

For our part, we must not prejudge the case. We must not assume that selfish or unselfish behavior is either good or bad until we actually determine where the truth exists. It may be that at certain times, selfish behavior is good, and at other times, it is bad. It also may be that unselfish behavior is sometimes good and at other times bad.

To summarize, we must understand that to bring the problem of selfishness and human nature into the jurisdiction of science, we must first develop an appropriate vocabulary with more precise, meaningful definitions. Second, to avoid any prejudging of the case we must eliminate the presence of value-judgments when formulating these definitions and words. We must employ a more objective, nonvalued terminology.

THE ARGUMENT FROM ANIMAL STUDIES

Very frequently, those who have sought to present in writing the notion that human beings are basically selfish or unselfish have pointed to animal behavior to buttress their viewpoint. Sometimes such writers have pointed to the behavior of the ancient "caveman" rather than animals. This situation has been especially true for philosophers, theologians, and political theorists. It is really absurd how often such writers have turned to the proverbial jungle—to the wolf, tiger, lion, and other such animals—in an effort to bolster their contention that human beings cannot be trusted.

Why is this so absurd? Because even on theoretical grounds, such theorizing is completely invalid. We can never make meaningful statements about human nature by arguing on the basis of other species' behavior. Indeed, what may be true for the characteristics of one animal species may be the precise opposite for another. Therefore, the intellectual approach of such theorists should not be labeled as Darwinian but rather as *pseudo-Darwinian*. It is true that psychologists will cite animal research for a variety of purposes, but when they are cautious, psychologists will admit that they are relying on animal research for only the preliminary study of a problem or the refinement of an experimental technique, rather than for uncovering scientific truth about human traits or qualities.

But this is not the place for a detailed analysis of pseudo-Darwinianism and its fundamental mistake. It is sufficient to say that its fallacy has been demonstrated well enough so that no repetition is required.

In any event, the pseudo-Darwinian approach can lead to conclusions about human nature quite different than its exponents typically suggest. What do I mean by this? For instance, instead of comparing the human being with the wolf or tiger, why not make the comparison with the rabbit or deer?

Instead of comparing human beings with carnivorous animals, why not compare them with the herbivorous? It is simple to point out that most of such pseudo-Darwinian comparisons involve only a few animal species out of the multitude that exist on earth.

Far more important is the argument that if we compare ourselves with our closest animal relatives—mainly the ape and especially the chimpanzee whom we know more about—then any biological inheritances seem less in the direction of selfishness, cruelty, domination, and tyranny than in the direction of cooperation, friendship, and unselfishness. For the latter is generally the way that chimpanzees behave.

In addition to observational data in the wild, there now exist some experimental data to support that statement. For instance, various experiments have demonstrated that chimpanzees will help their peers, such as giving of their own food when their neighbor is starving. The stronger chimpanzee is the protector rather than the dominator of the weaker.

It is also known by those who have worked with these animals that they can form what appear to be true friendships—even love relationships—not only with other chimpanzees but also with the human beings who work with them.

But I do not wish to make too much of such anecdotal observations. As I have suggested earlier, this whole line of argument is ultimately invalid anyway. However, I find it difficult to resist the poetic justice of "turning the tables" on the pseudo-Darwinianists by pointing to examples of unselfish, even altruistic, behavior in other animal species. Such a position effectively undercuts their argument that by studying other species, we can accurately conclude that human nature is essentially selfish, cruel, or domineering.

I would like to make a final point, and it concerns the prehistoric caveman. Typically, the cave dweller is presented as crude, cruel, aggressive, and even characteristically vicious. But there is absolutely no evidence whatsoever for this viewpoint. Virtually the only thing that scientists know about the prehistoric cave dweller is anatomy and nothing more. It always has been assumed that because the cave dweller *looked* brutish, he therefore behaved brutishly. Yet, it is quite possible that the cave dwellers were actually nicer— that is, more altruistic—toward one another than we are today in our civilization. I would not affirm this statement as necessarily true, but based on our limited knowledge, it is equally invalid to insist that the cave dwellers were cruel or vicious.

Let's admit that we know nothing at all about the cave dwellers. Popular depictions showing them wielding clubs on their family members or friends are just fanciful legends and not in the least derived from scientific truth. In assessing human nature with regard to selfishness, we must, therefore, reject all appeals to animal behavior or putative cave dweller behavior. They have no place in the debate in which we are now engaging.

"HEALTHY SELFISHNESS"

I have earlier pointed out that the words selfish and unselfish have attached to them values of varying kinds; that is, they are invidious words, to some extent prejudging the case. If it is possible to label something as selfish, then people typically will assume they should be against it and disapprove of it. But there have been psychiatric and clinical developments that make it necessary for us to reject as simplistic such an approach.

For instance, research on masochism clearly shows that a good deal of what appears to be unselfish behavior may come out of forces that are psychopathological and that originate in selfish motivation. We must not always take unselfish behavior as its face value, for it may cover up a good deal of hostility, jealousy, and even hatred. Unselfish behavior that arises from such motivations—that is, put on for a purpose—must certainly be considered as psychopathology.

In the process of psychotherapy, it is also necessary to teach such people to behave—at least at certain times—in what might be termed a healthfully selfish manner. Persons who lack self-respect and who reject their own basic impulses have to be taught a whole new way of thinking about themselves, because psychological health can only be achieved in this direction. In other words, from the psychiatric perspective, to do something for other people at the cost of self-deprivation is not always desirable.

The psychoanalyst Erich Fromm (1939) has put matters succinctly by saying that a person who has no self-respect or self-love cannot feel any real respect or love for others. Therefore, it is necessary to differentiate between healthy selfishness and unhealthy selfishness as well as between healthy unselfishness and unhealthy unselfishness. More specifically, we can say that there must be some differentiation between the behavior and motivation behind that behavior. The outward behavior may seem to be selfish or unselfish but so may the motivation that drives it.

This general conclusion is supported in a rather vague way by clinical experience regarding psychologically healthy and neurotic people. It may be fairly said that generally a correlation exists between psychological health and unselfish behavior. But the correlation goes much higher if we can differentiate the behavior from the motivation and say more accurately then that a very high correlation exists between psychological health and what we have called healthy unselfishness.

An examination of such emotionally healthy persons shows that when they behave unselfishly, this behavior tends to be a phenomenon of personal abundance stemming from relative basic gratification. It comes out of inner riches rather than inner poverty. The same kind of examination of neurotic persons will show that their selfish behavior is typically a phenomenon of basic deprivation involving threat, insecurity, and inner poverty.

It is commonplace for the clinician to assume that selfish, hostile, or nasty behavior generally arises from some insult or damage to the individual's own basic needs. It is ordinarily expected to be a phenomenon of thwarting, frustration, and conflict, whether arising in the past or the present.

So again, we end up with a new vocabulary. We may speak of the unselfishness of psychological abundance and the selfishness of psychological poverty.

OBSERVATIONS IN CHILDREN

It is possible to see very clearly in children the phenomenon that we have been describing. Unfortunately, it is usually accepted without further investigation that children are primarily selfish, much more so than adults. How such a conclusion could ever have been reached is hard to fathom, because even the most casual observation of children—at least of those who are emotionally healthy—will reveal many examples of truly altruistic, generous, unselfish behavior. Indeed, youngsters who are raised well and who are psychologically sound are apt to present to their parents problems related to unselfishness as often as selfishness. For example, such children are as likely to give away their expensive toys as to snatch these same toys away from peers.

Children's altruism has not been experimentally tested because admittedly it is difficult to measure. But this obstacle hardly negates the definite presence of unselfish traits in youngsters. Clearly, there is a lot of evidence already amassed to suggest that humans have a strong, inborn capacity for unselfishness.

During the mid-1960s, Maslow became quite favorably impressed with the relevance of European existentialism for humanistic psychology. Alongside such figures within the United States as Rollo May and Carl Rogers, Maslow came to value existentialism as a philosophically important movement for psychological theory and psychotherapy. In this brief, unpublished paper dated February 8, 1966, he set forth his viewpoint.

20

Science, Psychology, and the Existential Outlook

We are in a period of transition from one image of the human being to another, from one philosophy of life to another. The old one might be called the mechanosomorphic image of humanity and of social science. The new image is that of humanistic philosophy. Some call it the neo-humanistic view. Others have termed it the neo-neo-humanistic or even the neo-neo-neo humanistic—with no end in sight. It is like talking about a future way of perceiving and attempting to do so in terms of the only vocabulary we have, a vocabulary that is now being replaced. This becomes a difficult problem in description.

As a general statement, it may be called the humanistic worldview of life, particularly regarding human nature. All the behavioral sciences are being affected. Some of the writers espousing this viewpoint are Lewis Mumford and the contributors to the *Journal of Humanistic Psychology*. Aldous Huxley also was trying to express this viewpoint at the time of his death. It is a rejection of the nonhuman, impersonal, object-oriented approach.

One recent book with this outlook is Floyd Matson's (1966) *The Broken Image*. Another book that you will have to read sentence by sentence and then reread—it took me 4 months to get through it, and now I am rereading it—is Michael Polyani's (1964) *Science, Faith, and Society.* This is a work that everyone in the behavioral sciences will have to read.

What is happening in this worldwide "two-party" system of scientific outlook? What is happening in psychology? The mechanistic viewpoint in science, the behaviorist image of human beings, treats the individual as a passive thing, akin to a billiard ball on a billiard table. In contrast, we have within psychology a lot of splinter groups—for example, those following the teachings of Theodre Reik, Alfred Adler, or others—united previously only in their criticism of the mechanistic viewpoint. Recently, the major force in cementing these disparate groups has been the influence of European existentialism, taken over and Americanized by thinkers in our country. This situation has occurred just in the past 3 or 4 years.

The "new existentialism" contrasts the image of the human being as a passive object dominated by Marxian economic forces or Freudian unconscious forces with the image instead of the human being as a mover.

Today, there is also much new talk about choice, personal experience, decision, and responsibility. There is much writing about the way in which it is possible to be your own boss, to take your fate into your own hands. In B. F. Skinner's writings (and Skinner is the smartest of the behaviorists), you will never find these words. Rather, he constantly talks about reinforcement.

In Skinner's (1962) novel, *Walden Two,* the entire population is treated by conditioning, shaping, and molding. Essentially, it is a passive society led by a benevolent prophet. But Skinner never tells us who molds the prophet. Nor does Skinner explain what would happen if the prophet were not benevolent but instead malevolent. In contrast, the existentialist approach emphasizes the ability of each person to choose and to resist suggestion by others. Significantly, this picture leads to new kinds of social science research.

Today, there is a great deal of talk about the self and about personal identity. What is implied by such discussion is something we can call *"humanness,"* but among the mechanistic thinkers, there is no such notion of human nature. For existentialists, something is *there* to be uncovered. The existentialist is the agent, the self-mover, the decider.

The new psychology also has a philosophy of health and sickness. What do I mean? Namely, that sickness comes from the denial of human potential.

The good life is the seeking of this potential and daily leading the life that it encourages. This approach concerns the higher possibilities of human beings—the way we all differ from chimpanzees or apes. The existentialist says that sickness would come from not living the higher life. It would come from human diminution rather than from invasion by bacteria or by external damage to our various organs.

This attitude generates too a philosophy of society. The good society is the one that fulfills the highest degree of human growth, of extending the highest aspects of human beings. Each of society's institutions might be so described.

For example, a religion from this perspective might well be productive or it might be psychopathogenic.

Science is the production of the scientist's own nature. And, it is a truism that this impersonal model originally comes from the physicist. Such a perspective is limited, inadequate, and sometimes even destructive. But these limitations are not necessary. In general, science can become humanistic. The impersonal model cannot be concerned with values, individuality, ethics, and morals. But in principle, science could be capable of value-laden directions.

The higher reaches of human nature are unexplainable by mechanistic psychology. The classic models break down when we attempt to study the higher kinds of people. Whenever I try to discuss this issue with my scientific friends, they ask, "Why are you trying to destroy science? Why do you hate science?" But the humanist does not hate science. I see my efforts as a means to enlarge science and to give it a wider jurisdiction. For there are certain kinds of data that simply cannot be handled by classic science. This notion has long been understood by novelists, poets, and religious people. They all have a fear of science, a fear that many young people today share. Indeed, many persons believe that if every nuclear scientist were to drop dead instantly, it would be a good thing. Such persons believe that science is a threat to what is beautiful and awe-inspiring in life.

This seemingly irrational viewpoint has its undeniably justifiable aspects. Mainstream science has a need to desacrilize. It is used as a tool to negate the sacred and emotionality, and I think this is done deliberately. My psychological research offers examples of this situation, but I will present an autobiographical account: my first operation in medical school at the University of Wisconsin.

I think our professor deliberately tried to harden us. He conveyed no sensibility to us that the operation was being performed to help a fellow human being. The patient was regarded as a thing, an object. The operation was intended to remove a cancerous breast, and it was done callously. Our professor used a cauterizing knife that burned the flesh. He cut in a design as though performing embroidery on a piece of cloth. The resultant smell was like burning steak. Our professor paid no attention to the students who were vomiting or fainting all around him. He tossed the woman's severed breast onto the counter where it landed with a "plop" that I can still hear after more than 30 years.

I attended medical school for only a year before quitting. I objected to its lack of reverence for the sacredness of life and death. Unfortunately, the medical students themselves tried to live up to the school's ideal of emotional "toughness." No one told me who the person had been whose body I was to dissect. I had to find out myself that he had been a timber worker and learn how he had died. Instead of referring to these as people who had died, they were simply called cadavers. The medical students tried to prove how unfeeling they were by having their photographs taken while seated on their cadavers and eating sandwiches. The students also enjoyed talking to outsiders, especially women, and then casually pulling from their trouser pockets a cadaverous hand or foot.

Instead of this desacrilizing and technological approach, wouldn't a more priestly, human approach be helpful to medicine today? The effort of medical science to desacrilize our higher emotions is an attempt to abort all awe and wonder. It is a reductive attitude—the "nothing but" perspective: "A human being is nothing but $24 worth of chemicals." Or, "A kiss is nothing but the juxtaposition of the upper ends of two gastroalimentary canals." I have accumulated dozens of such examples. For some reason, I find these amusing.

One more example: I have a friend who had a brush with death. He underwent a critical operation, and there was a good chance that he would die. He told me about the experience, which was tremendously emotional and awesome. Really, it was mystical. He saw visions, he saw his whole life clearly, and then he made resolutions. This all happened about 2 years ago, and since then, he has lived very differently. Something very profound obviously happened during his operative experience. After I talked with my friend, I decided that such experiences ought to be researched, for instance, right there in the operating room setting.

Soon afterward, I asked a surgeon if my friend's experience was at all typical, and he dismissively replied: "Oh, sure. Very common. Demerol, you know." That was his entire comment!

Now, is it the intrinsic nature of science to desacrilize the world in this way? I doubt it, for really great scientists do not do so. They have genuine tenderness, humility, and a sense of awe. But most of such scientists are very shy about expressing these kinds of feelings. Perhaps science can rid itself of the threat to tenderness only if scientists know they will not be ridiculed. For this to happen, we will need to change our entire outlook.

During the mid-1950s, Maslow was interested in collaborating on a comprehensive text to encompass all of modern psychology. It would not be a shallow introductory book but rather a sophisticated and value-driven treatise—along the lines of William James's (1890, 1981) seminal The Principles of Psychology—*that might help to revitalize academic psychology and thereby create a better world. Maslow finally abandoned this project after deciding that the field had grown so much since his undergraduate years in the 1920s that such a single volume was no longer feasible. He intended this brief, undated paper to serve as the book's preface.*

21

What Psychology Can Offer the World

Some scientists unfortunately resemble religious fundamentalists who believe that there is only one way to reach heaven. Thus, some scientists stress quantification as the key to the divine kingdom. Or rather peculiarly, they may emphasize impracticality—that is, any research that might conceivably benefit humanity is dismissed as totally "unscientific." Many scientists essentially sanctify one particular brand of experimental technique and sneer at all the others. These people sometimes remind me of religious schismatics, who are so absorbed in pronouncing the sacred prayer correctly—or in observing the holy ritual in precisely the right manner—that they forget what the whole matter was spiritually about in the first place.

For the authentic scientist rather than the technician, religion is a way of reaching the truth, understanding the world, and answering the questions posed by an insistent humanity. The others are just scientific Pharisees, who love the *style* of doing something more than what is actually being done.

In this time of all times, the possibility for complete catastrophe threatens all humanity. Yet, utopia seems to beckon ever more brightly. Therefore, I feel justified more than ever in turning again with the most severe and dignified dedication, to ask seriously and without cynicism, cant or self-consciousness: What is the meaning of life? How can we best achieve happiness and serenity? How can we become fine people, sincere, honest, and good? How can we attain that of which we are capable? What can we reasonably ask of human nature, and what puts too great a strain on it? What can human nature demand of society? How can we change society to make all these things possible?

If psychology today cannot give better answers to these questions than could be given 50 years ago by the wisest people alive, then it has failed as a field. But I believe psychology *can* give better answers to these questions than has ever been possible before. More than that, I believe that the hope of the world lies in understanding the nature of society—that is, through all the social sciences and particularly through psychology.

I have tried to keep fresh and naive all my original, adolescent awe, wonder, and curiosity—as well as the concern with the basic problems of life, love, and happiness with which I began all my studies as a boy. Because I am sincerely convinced that the already extant literature of psychology has many materials for the answers to humanity's universal and timeless questions, I have fixed my attention on precisely these materials.

In so doing, I have summarily and without apology neglected many of the problems, experiments, and techniques of social science that chiefly resemble the esoteric appurtenances of a Greek-letter society or social "lodge." Their purpose seems more to bolster the self-esteem of its members and set them apart from ordinary people than to serve the guiding principles of public servants who stand humbly in the same line with the great questioners and answerers of all time: Aristotle, Socrates, Descartes, and Spinoza, and modern psychological thinkers like William James, Sigmund Freud, and Max Wertheimer. Throughout my career, this has been my goal.

ఴ During the late 1960s, Maslow became increasingly disturbed by how the intellectual establishment in the United States was neglecting humanistic psychology and its growing impact on counseling and psychotherapy, education, management, and organizational development. Indeed, his own influential writings were almost completely—and seemingly willfully—ignored by the media elite. In this unpublished essay written in February 1969, Maslow expressed strong sentiments on this subject.

22

The Unnoticed
Psychological Revolution

These are some notes I am setting down for possibly writing an article to appear in a mass-circulation magazine. For several years, I have thought about doing such a piece, but I just have no taste for popular writing, and I have always avoided the task. But now it occurs to me that first of all, I must and should do it. For nobody else is doing it.

What started me off this morning was finishing historian Frank Manuel's (1968) new book, *A Portrait of Isaac Newton*. Manuel ended his volume without at all recognizing the existence of humanistic science. In conversing about the subject, I have decided to make a lecture out of my ideas or else a chapter in my planned book on the propositions of humanistic psychology.[1] That is what I think I will do. I will begin the next semester by presenting a lecture on the humanistic revolution in contemporary psychology and science.

And I have been ruminating about these disgusting magazines whose subscriptions I am going to cancel: *The Atlantic Monthly, Harper's, The Saturday Review* (that is the best of them, but it's not very good), and the *New York Review of Books* (which is definitely the worst). All of these mass-circulation periodicals reveal the entire intellectual establishment's alienation and its total lack of knowledge about the emerging new intellectual synthesis. I was thinking this morning: Where are the great names from among the humanists today? These magazines never even mention them. Where are Carl Rogers, Gordon Allport, Henry Murray, and Gardner Murphy, let alone the younger people like Michael Murphy (founder-director of the Esalen Institute)?

Why didn't Frank Manuel (1968) discuss at all the post-Newtonian synthesis in science highlighted by contemporary philosophers like Michael Polyani and myself? Why aren't the books of the humanistic psychologists ever mentioned, let alone the writings of the relatively few humanistic economists, political philosophers, and sociologists? Their books simply aren't noticed. For example, none of my books has ever been reviewed in any of the popular magazines or newspapers like the *New York Times*.

A sad thing about this whole business is that we can interpret one aspect of the radical youth rebellion and the black rebellion as a reaching-out for precisely this humanistic personal ethic and philosophy. They reach out for it as if it this system didn't already exist. Yet, it does exist. The political rebels just don't know about it. In a way, we could call this humanistic system an answer to their prayers and demands. In principle, it is something that should satisfy these rebels, because it is a system of values that involves a reconstruction of science as a means of discovering and uncovering values (rather than allowing it to be value-free).

Not only for this reason is humanistic psychology relevant, but also because it includes the beginnings of a strategy and set of tactics for attaining these worthy ends. That is, it offers a theory of education, including a philosophy of educational means and ends. The same holds true for politics and economics. That is, we can talk about moral, humanistic, or *eupsychian* politics and economics—and divide this discussion into one of ultimate goals and values on the one hand and strategy, tactics, and means on the other.

For example, if I had the desire and the time, I could construct a system of *Being-art,* that is, of art as exposing the transcendental realm of Being and actively fostering *peak-experiences* and *plateau-experiences.* In other words, I could develop a system of art to improve human beings or at least to expose people to the world of higher values, which it is certainly possible to attain. Something similar could be said for music too, as indicated in my published article on music education (see Maslow, 1968a).

True enough, there is hardly a single philosopher I could cite in this context except in bits and pieces. But then, this whole system that I am constructing composes a comprehensive philosophy of life, a philosophy of everything, so that a psychological or philosophical system of Being-art also could be created to encompass poetry, the novel, drama, and the verbal arts. All of these would possess the same goals, strategy, and tactics—the same intrinsic values and the same transpersonal usefulness—for humankind. That is, art in general can be seen as a growth-fostering realm and as offering a path toward self-actualization and humanness-fulfillment.

Of course, I must raise the question of statistics here. That is, how many people today actually are touched by this new humanistic synthesis? Then consider the following: How many *more* could be touched by it, supposing there were adequate publicity and appropriate statements in mass-circulation magazines and newspapers, radio, and television? Yet, in thinking about statistics and numbers, the answer from history is rather clear: We can expect that growth initially involves 1% of this generation reaching out to the corresponding 1% of the next generation. We also would anticipate a fair amount of misunderstanding, misinterpretation, and lack of clarity about our movement.

But this confusion is inevitable. The growing tip always involves a small proportion of humankind, yet it will carry on. As a matter of fact, that is precisely what is happening with the whole humanistic synthesis right now: The actual groundbreaking is being done by a few people, and most of the other humanistic-espousing material currently being generated is just routine, mediocre, or even outright crap. That is all part of the game, and there is no way of avoiding it so long as human beings are human beings.

One big point is that whatever the statistics on influence may turn out to be—concerning the pace in which this viewpoint is accepted, supported, and validated—it is still terribly important that this humanistic system exists. Why? Because it is the vital antidote for the hopelessness and pessimism that currently pervade our society's intellectual class. Specifically, I am referring to all those people, young and adult, who can only criticize and protest and who see no positive reconstruction and transcending synthesis that goes beyond what presently exists.

In part, this is what I mean by the growing tip of the next generation. And, for the nonpsychological groups throughout the present generation, it is necessary that they be given a vision of at least the possibility—if not the certainty—that there is a leap forward possible, a viable theory of social improvement or social revolution, in short, that there is a possibility for envisaging a good society.

For it is not true that human society must inevitably be bad, as the anarchists vociferously argue. Nor is it inevitable, as so many theologians and left-wing/right-wing political radicals proclaim, that human nature is inherently evil and incapable of growing into something better. The humanistic and transpersonal synthesis of psychology today knocks these ideas on their head or, at least, strongly contradicts them.

I would guess that the more zestful, cheerful, life-positive, hopeful, and optimistic people now existing and who will exist in the next generation will seize on this new psychological revolution even though its tenets are not yet verified sufficiently: Such people will act on it, live by it, and work at it. And, of course, that is very much what this revolution needs: workers, in all the fields, encompassing the scientific, professional, and applied. Something like this energy is also necessary in the recesses of one's own, private, subjective mind in order to give one the courage and hope to continue and work toward something better.

It can be emphasized that the whole humanistic synthesis resembles a smorgasbord: a big table offering all sorts of ways of life. In this manner, people could choose the particular paths that they find appealing and that resonate with their unique interests, perceptions, and tastes. Thus, art as a path toward self-actualization would not work for everyone. It would leave some persons cold, but it would certainly be effective for those who are aesthetically sensitive or inclined. The same principle would hold true for music or for the mesomorphic way of body athletics such as dancing. After all, there are many *Being-values,* and anyone can enter into the *Being-realm* via any single one of these—whether beauty, truth, virtue, perfection, or whatever it might be.

EDITOR'S NOTE

1. Maslow never wrote this book, nor was there even a manuscript.

PART III

Management, Organizations, and Social Change

↩ *During the late 1960s, Maslow became increasingly disturbed about the growing trend toward self-indulgence and hedonism among many allying themselves loosely with humanistic psychology. Though various "growth centers" were flourishing around the United States, he viewed with definite uneasiness their emphasis on self-expression as the key to healthy personality functioning. Certainly, the most famous of these growth centers was the Esalen Institute at scenic Big Sur, California. For several years, Maslow had periodically led seminars there. But in this unpublished article dated March 20, 1970, he offered a trenchant critique of the Esalen Institute and what it had come to espouse since its founding a decade earlier.*

23

Beyond Spontaneity

A Critique of the Esalen Institute

What are the next steps for humanistic psychology today? Beyond sensory awareness, spontaneity, body relaxation, and personal expressiveness—then what? Certainly, all of these aforementioned features of daily life produce no final heaven.

It has become necessary to criticize how impulsivity is being mistaken for spontaneity.

We must evaluate the Esalen Institute according to its products, that is, people. It must be evaluated in the same way that any other educational or therapeutic institution must be evaluated.

We must beware of people at growth centers like Esalen who are anti-intellectual, anti-rational, anti-scientific, and anti-research. We must regard experientialism as only a means to further ends, even though it is also an end-experience in itself. Certainly, experientialism is good in itself, but it is not enough. We must continue beyond that quality to seek knowledge, values, and wisdom. Why is there no library at Esalen?

We must join health psychology with sickness psychology. Esalen should not exclude the insights of Sigmund Freud and psychoanalysis.

There needs to be a better balance at Esalen between the Dionysian and the Apollonian. There needs to be more dignity, politeness, courtesy, reserve, privacy, responsibility, and loyalty. There should be much less talk about "instant intimacy" and "instant love" and much more about the necessity for Apollonian controls such as pace and style.

At places like the Esalen Institute, there must be more stress on work, discipline, and lifelong effort. The ladder of consciousness must be climbed gradually, step by step.

It is important to differentiate between *peak-experiences* and *plateau-experiences,* between the flash of insight and the patient working-through of self-knowledge and between psychedelic experience and psychotherapy. Esalen staff members tend to view human personality growth in terms of the "big bang" of tremendous inner breakthroughs, but true growth is rather a lifelong task.

The notion advocated by many at Esalen of "consciousness for consciousness's sake" must be criticized and rejected. This notion has all the inherent evil of "art for art's sake," or "science for science's sake," or "high intelligence for high intelligence's sake." The essential point is that all such philosophies are amoral.

The various *Being-values* must be determined in terms of each other, or else they can lead to the evil results that have arisen in the psychedelic or hippie movement today. With these movements, people tend to search for and value anything that will produce another intense experience or alteration of ordinary consciousness. Historically, this ideology has always led in mystical movements to a kind of selfishness—that is, in using other people simply as a means to alter one's consciousness rather than to enter into what Martin Buber has called an *I-thou relationship* with them. Such an outlook has usually led to magic and a fascination for such arcana as astrology, card reading, and numerology.

In turn, these activities historically have led to an antirationalism, anti-intellectualism, anti-science, and, finally, an anti-fact. And then, these viewpoints ultimately have led into sadism because sadism may give "new experiences" and may "turn some people on." In any case, with the "consciousness for consciousness's sake" mystique, there are no principles by which to criticize an alteration of consciousness, that is, to say whether it is good or evil or whether it causes good or evil.

The final product of this whole line of ideological development can be a death-wish, because dying, suicide, and killing can, in themselves, produce "new experiences." The sado-masochistic literature is filled with examples of this attitudinal sequence. The English author Colin Wilson (1959) has written about such cases. For instance, men who are put to death by hanging sometimes involuntarily display an erection followed by ejaculation at the last instant before dying. Therefore, some masochists try to nearly hang themselves in order to achieve this same intense experience. This example vividly shows the final windup of all this in evil and death.

In any discussion, growth centers like the Esalen Institute must always be judged by their actual products and not simply by their seemingly well-meaning intentions. To put it most succinctly, do places like Esalen make good persons or bad persons? Do they make our society better or worse?

In the last few years of Maslow's life, he became increasingly interested in the use of applied techniques to enhance our empathic and social skills. In this regard, he found t-groups (i.e., "sensitivity-training" groups originally developed by counseling leaders like Carl Rogers) to be extremely effective. In this unpublished article written about 1970, Maslow set forth his ideas on the important potential of t-groups in creating greater global harmony.

24

Building Community Through T-Groups

In approaching the entire subject of catalyzing humanistic political and social change in the world today, I am starting with the following principles:

1. All human beings compose a single species.

2. Any differences found among individuals within our species are less basic and less important than the similarities. This notion applies even for such seemingly significant categories as male-female, old-young, intelligent-unintelligent, and race.

3. Not only is it biologically and psychologically *possible* for our entire species to be organized into a universal brotherhood/sisterhood—a species-wide political unit—but also that,

4. The practical situation today—that is, the existence of enormous weapons of destruction that could destroy our whole species or set it back terri-

bly—makes specieswide politics an urgent, imperative situation. In effect, we are all living in a state of emergency that calls for a "crash" program.

5. Level-three politics provides a framework for moving purposefully and efficiently toward specieswide political endeavors while maintaining sufficient order, stability, and continuation of services so that World War III can be averted (I call this *homeostatic politics*).

6. At every level, current politics is atomistic rather than holistic, as it must become. The most significant example of atomism is that of national sovereignty, which I conceive to be the primary condition for war and the certain guarantee that future wars *will* come. The main task of humanistic politics is to transcend—not abolish—national sovereignty in favor of a more inclusive, specieswide politics.

7. The atomism, separatism, and mutual exclusiveness of national sovereignty must be seen as systematic of our civilization rather than symptomatic. That is, the atomistic and separative way of cognizing, valuing, socializing, and acting today is deeply embedded in the blood and bones of most (though not all) people everywhere. This atomizing pervades all aspects of life, all interpersonal relationships, intrapsychic relationships, our relations to nature and to the physical world, even our (Aristotelian) logic and (analytically oriented) science and our most basic conceptions of love, marriage, friendship, and family. We often unconsciously view such relationships as adversarial, zero-sum, or counter-synergic; that is, one must either dominate or be dominated or that "My advantage must be your disadvantage."

But even when this mutual exclusiveness between two individuals, or within members of a family is transcended so that all become a holistic One, such an achievement most frequently is accomplished at the cost of making the family, club, clan, tribe, socioeconomic class, nationality, religion, or racial group into an internally coherent, friendly, loyal, cooperative, and needs-pooling entity by making it mutually exclusive from the rest of the world. The sociobiologist Robert Ardrey (1966) has aptly termed this phenomenon the *amity-enmity complex.*

That is, the main technique that humanity has used until now for achieving amity within a group is to regard all nongroup members—the "they"—as more or less an enemy. Individuals within the group become allies because they share a common enemy—if not a life-threatening or dangerous enemy, then one about which to feel superior, contemptuous, condescending, or insulting. To me, the ultimate absurdity seems to be that this phenomenon seems to hold true for most peace/antiwar organizations (though with a few honorable exceptions).

All polarizing, splitting, excluding, dominating, hurting, hating, insulting, anger-producing, vengefulness-producing, and put-down techniques are atomistic rather than holistic. Therefore, these serve to separate humankind into mutually hostile groups. These methods are countergrowth and make specieswide politics less possible, thereby postponing the attainment of one world law and government. To put it starkly, these techniques are war fostering and peace delaying.

8. Moving toward specieshood and specieswide politics necessarily means a profound holisticizing of ourselves—for each of us—of our interpersonal relationships, subcultures within societies and nations, and our relationships with not only our own species but with other species as well and with nature and the cosmos as a whole. This process means moving toward holism in all the professions, for example, away from adversarial law, adversarial politics, and adversarial economics. It also means abandoning our atomistic way of attempting to separate knowledge into mutually exclusive jurisdictions, departments, fields, or "turfs" as do many trade unions or juvenile gangs. This relinquishing of turfs also must occur for each of our social and educational institutions, religions, work and managerial settings, and administrations of justice.

Against this overcondensed background, each sentence of which requires expanding and implementing, I wish to make one specific proposal, namely, that *t-groups* (encounter groups, sensitivity training, etc.) as well as various techniques used by human growth centers and described as "Esalen-type education" be used toward holisticizing our society and eventually the entire world. Of course, this process already has been initiated by National Training Laboratories (NTL) in its mix-max groups, that is, forming t-groups out of people who are as *diverse* as possible. But I think that it is possible to accomplish even more in this direction. The black-white (racial) confrontation groups provide a better example of what I mean.

Most of all, I would suggest a thorough reexamination of the widely accepted principle of homogamy. For example, a lot of data now indicates that the more alike people are in their background, socioeconomic class, caste, religion, national origin, and educational attainment, the more likely their marriage will be happy and endure. This principle, therefore, is assumed to be true for all interpersonal relationships, such as friendships, business partnerships, and neighborhood connections.

It is obviously true that we feel more comfortable and relaxed—less tense, uneasy, and uncertain—and less suspicious, paranoid, alien, or wary with someone who shares our tastes, folkways, and prejudices. It is obviously easier to organize our lives so as to maximize contact with those who are similar and to minimize contact with those who are dissimilar.

But if we accept the necessity for holisticizing humankind, then this way of making our lives easier and more comfortable can be seen as a cop-out, a weak attempt at fleeing the uncomfortable but necessary decision. The big question is, If we wish to move toward specieshood and universalism, how do we overcome our separative and encapsulating social behaviors?

How can we transcend the differences that now compartmentalize humankind into mutually exclusive, isolated groups that have nothing to do with each other? How can we make contact *across* the walls that divide socioeconomic classes, religions, races, nationalities, tribes, professional groups, and IQ groups?

Obviously, if we all agreed that ending racial enmity was a tremendous and urgent necessity requiring a crash program, then we could solve this problem quite easily—at least, in principle, by legalizing or subsidizing *only* interracial marriages. In the same way, interreligious, intertribal, and international marriages could homogenize the population. One day, the emergency caused by factionalism may become so great that such measures may *have* to be attempted. For instance, many people have suggested that the United States and the Soviet Union exchange large numbers of their children to guarantee that each nation won't bomb the other.

However, much more practical for the general purpose of transcending homogamy would be the widespread use of t-groups as a holistic-political tool. There is already enough clinical experience with black-white (racial) t-groups so that we can begin to try out the same principle with all other separated groups.

I am not suggesting the t-group technique so much as a panacea as that it happens to be available—that is, already widely used and accepted with an already functioning apparatus of teaching institutions, trained practitioners, and international contacts.

In principle, it would be wise to keep the end-goal, rather than any specific method, carefully in mind: the brotherhood/sisterhood of all human beings. From this perspective, any technique is good if it fosters greater communication, understanding, inclusiveness, intimacy, trust, openness, honesty, self-exposure, feedback, identification, closeness, compassion, tolerance, acceptance, friendliness, and love. Conversely, any technique is good if it reduces suspicion, paranoid expectation, fear, enmity, defensiveness, contemptuousness, condescension, polarization, splitting, alienation, foreignness, separation, exclusion, and hatred.

◖ Though Abraham Maslow is probably best known for his theories on individual motivation and personality growth, he was hardly indifferent to societal problems. During the 1960s, Maslow became dismayed by the steady erosion of friendship and intimacy in contemporary Western society. In this unpublished paper written in April 1968, Maslow raised a series of important questions to guide our thinking concerning the creation of true community.

25

Fostering Friendship, Intimacy, and Community

The major question facing us today is how to learn to be intimate and to overcome alienation and distancing among people. I agree with Jerry Sohl (1967) in his book *The Lemon Eaters* that one of the main causes for this situation is the breakup of the permanent and enduring, face-to-face relationships common in the past, at least in rural areas, villages, extended families and clans, and *real* neighborhoods.

In my book *Eupsychian Management: A Journal* (Maslow, 1965), I observed that *t-groups* are essentially intimacy groups. They teach, or try to teach, people to recover the enduring, stable, long-term, and undivorceable relationships that previous generations enjoyed with their relatives, neighbors, and people in the next farm or village. Nowadays, we have almost exclusively the isolated nuclear family composed of only two generations.

It is this social-emotional problem today with which any utopian or *eupsychian* thinker must grapple. People feel unfulfilled in their basic need for togetherness, closeness, or deeply rooted relationships that are beyond divorce and conceived to be lifelong, with various duties and responsibilities as well as pleasures.

Certainly, some encouraging examples already exist. I think of the California industrialist Andrew Kay and his Unitarian fellowships that are permanent in nature. Also, I admire the weekly luncheon meeting of the dozen or so humanistic psychotherapists in Los Angeles who become closer and closer to one another in this way.

How can we re-create the positive aspects of the old Greek letter fraternities and sororities and the local church congregations? Is it possible to organize our society at its base in terms of such extended groups? Is it possible to have groups of perhaps 20 or 40 people somehow keep touch with one another, just as close-knit relatives in the past have done? How can this situation be accomplished in our highly mobile society? How can this goal be reconciled with the mass needs of an industrial civilization that casually transfers employees from place to place?

We also must deal with the issue of how to overcome the divorce between the home and workplace that is so common among commuters today. Currently, children and spouses are divorced too from one's daily workplace. They are effectively denied access to an important part of their family members' daily life.

Can we organize colleges to foster a greater sense of community? Is it possible to establish suites, houses, fraternities, or the like in which 20 to 40 people share a common library or gathering place? Is it possible to keep such groups from dissolving? Perhaps, there can be some modification of the Bennington College arrangement of dividing student dormitories into houses that are small enough to permit intimacy and mutual knowledge to all the students and through which they can govern themselves.

How can we foster families that are more extended? Obviously, the first task would be to increase grandparent involvement with youngsters. I have no doubt that contemporary young adults—those below the age of 30 or maybe even 40—suffer from having been deprived as children of grandparental care. (For that matter, today's young adults were deprived of close parents, too.)

In this context, I recall my experience living in the same Brooklyn apartment building with my wife, two daughters, and many relatives and in-laws during the Depression. It was a very satisfying arrangement. Yet, such group closeness seems possible only when all the people are fairly decent and there is an individual who is willing to undergo a lot of personal trouble to be the "clan" mother or father and to hold the whole group together. Such group-living situations often fail due to the presence of mentally unstable people like paranoids, psychopaths, or authoritarian characters.

In a recent issue of *Encounter,* Leslie Fiedler (1968) makes a relevant observation on the subject of intimacy in discussing the huge expansion of tourism in Greece. He remarks that "tourism" contributes to alienation today of both the tourists and the people "toured" and stared at, that is, of both the spectators and the performers. Fiedler writes the following:

> They are quite as prepared to believe that pleasure is always somewhere other than home, as their grandparents were to believe that cultural uplift is invariably elsewhere. And the Greeks have caught on quickly, as they had to if they were not to perish. . . . They can sell their scenery and sunlight, their motherland and themselves so long as they keep singing and dancing and drinking in ways that tourists find "quaint," that is, ways that are less and less relevant to the world which they, as well as the tourists, actually inhabit. (p. 46)

The phenomenon of modern tourism offers another example of how people are distanced from each another—truly alienated in the sense of being made alien instead of intimate toward each other. For most people today, travel consists of being a spectator and a hurried one at that. They go to look at something instead of to "live" someplace, that is, to look at the new culture rather than to experience it. I think back to my summer fieldwork with the Canadian Blackfoot tribe in 1938. It probably comprised more real travel than most tourists do in 30 years of dashing around, simply staring at strange sights, and living with the "leeches" who thrive on tourists and keep them away from the real culture.

When I visited Mexico in the late 1950s, it was quite evident that there were really two cultures and two cities and that they had little to do with one another. There was the city in which ordinary Mexicans lived, ate, worked, and belonged. Then there was this foreign invasion of people who, in effect, were peeping Toms, spectators, and scopophiliacs. They were tourists in the worst sense of the term, and the word now has gained a bad connotation.

The problem is not only that the tourists do not really see anything meaningful and, therefore, do not really travel. That is, they corrupt the corruptible aspects of the culture at which they have come to stare. They actually harm the places that they visit. Ironically, tourists themselves are always talking about seeking places that are still "unspoiled"—meaning those areas that haven't yet been corrupted by spectators, tourists, passers-through, and alienated witnesses.

The managerial theorist Warren Bennis has suggested the possibility of quick and transient but authentic intimacy in a fast-paced society like ours. Certainly, this notion has real validity. For example, I know hundreds of people and can truthfully say that I have affection for all of them. I can enjoy traveling across the United States to spend a few hours with hundreds of people whom I could list, yet whom I might not see again for 3 or 4 years, or perhaps never, communicating only by an occasional letter.

But this situation exerts its psychological toll. In a certain sense, my friendships are, therefore, not deeply rooted except in my own mind. There are a fair number of these hundreds of "friends" whom I would enjoy having living next door, or in the same village, or within walking distance. Then, I suppose, we could develop the rich store of joint history, knowledge, and experience that would constitute a more vibrant intimacy than now exists among us.

Yet, it is important not to cast this issue in black-and-white terms. There are definite advantages in the fact that I have met personally and talked with, and at least occasionally been more or less close to, virtually everyone in the world who could be called my colleague, that is, all the leaders and main contributors to the field of psychology.

But there has to be something more geographically rooted about these interactions for them to be really satisfying. That is, my relationship with most of these friends is not of a next-door or drop-in or "see each other often" quality. Therefore, my relationship with the Rands, whom I do see on a neighborhood basis, differs fundamentally from my relationship with, say, Harry Murray, Warren Bennis, or even Henry Geiger, people whom I simply do not see very often no matter how good I feel about them or they about me.

I think it comes now to the necessity of having some equivalent of the old family organization as a center, from which can "fan out" all sorts of other work relationships, acquaintances, colleagues, friendships, and the like.

In any case, I think we all are gaining the viewpoint that our society, or any industrial society, has a sine qua non characteristic of destruction of intimacy and, therefore, a perpetual yearning for it and, consequently, various kinds of psychopathology that may result from this deprivation. I can use Jerry Sohl's (1967) *The Lemon Eaters* or any other good therapy or t-group collection of accounts as vivid case histories. That way, I can better discuss the widespread absence of social intimacy today and the methods available for recovering some sense of intimacy, candor, honesty, self-exposure, and feedback, and, then, the good results that follow.

During the late 1960s, Maslow was quite ambivalent about the American counterculture. Though sharing its ideals for a more altruistic, ethical, and just society, he regarded most of its adherents—especially the "hippies"—as intellectually lazy and often self-absorbed in a destructive way. Written in September 1969, this unpublished essay offers Maslow's thoughts on the higher values possible in the United States.

26

Defining the American Dream

In psychologist Lewis Yablonsky's (1968) last chapter of *Hippie Trip,* he is quite perceptive about the anomie afflicting many hippies and other young Americans. For many of today's youth, and certainly older people too, the dominant American value system is no longer gripping. They no longer feel unquestioning loyal to it. Therefore, our society's norms no longer control their actions and a state of anomie, normlessness, or what I have called *metapathology* now exists.

Yet, this troubling situation makes a certain undeniable sense. The truth is that the American dream is characteristically articulated in a very low or materialistic way. As a matter of fact, it is not even articulated very much by *anyone* nowadays. Perhaps the last important figure who really articulated the American dream well was Thomas Jefferson, living more than 140 years ago.

The way I would analyze the present, prevailing situation is to say that the American value system—the American dream—is typically expressed in *lower-need* terms (e.g., in terms of income) and almost entirely in materialistic terms. That is, personal success is generally defined in terms of the amount of money one receives and, along with it, the number of symbolic, status objects that one has attained in life, such as a fancy automobile, a boat, a big house in an upscale neighborhood, lavish vacations, and fine clothes.

But to enjoy a good life, *all* of these status objects are expendable. Not one of them is actually necessary for true fulfillment. Psychologists know that what *is* necessary for human nature is that, as our material gratifications are satisfied, we move upward in our needs through belongingness (community, brotherhood/sisterhood, friendliness), to love and affection, to achievement and competence with ensuing dignity and self-respect, and then on up to freedom for self-actualization and for expressing and resolving our unique idiosyncrasies. And then upward, still higher, to our *metaneeds* (the *Being-values*).

But where has this conception been at all meaningfully articulated? Which U.S. president or senator has even attempted to speak in such terms? For that matter, which contemporary professor or philosopher has attempted to speak in such terms? It is no wonder that so many young people today see the entire social system of the United States as geared to making them adopt a wholly materialistic definition of success in life.

And because their lower needs generally have been satisfied and they have been raised by good parents who were kind, loving, and respectful, these youth are ready for the Being-values, for self-actualization, for real discussions about love, affection, dignity, respect, and cooperation. Then, they look about our current society, and they do not hear any such talk. No governmental official is speaking in these crucial terms. There is no official track toward the attainment of these goals. As a matter of fact, they are not discussed as goals at all even by presidential committees on national goals—committees who would much rather talk about materialist matters such as the gross national product, economic growth, or the amount of goods turned out by industry.

In other words, the young adults today who are confronting American society are not being offered the *metavalues* as a formal goal. For them, the higher values are, therefore, not part of the formal U.S. value system. Consequently, these youth perceive the United States as a limited system of lower motivation, lower needs, lower aspirations, and lower goals that any self-respecting, mature human being would despise and reject. Anyway, the whole American dream thing today is phrased materialistically.

Moreover, there is no clear track in our society upward to the *B-values*. How many young adults have come to me and said, "I would like to lead a good life. What shall I do? Where shall I go?" Frequently, I do not quite know how to answer them. I think of nice young people whom I know—who acquire a taste of the higher life from a group experience or from an inspiring book. Logically enough, they want to have more of the same and to go further with their personal development. But what can I tell them? Where shall I send them? There simply is no clear track. There is no vocational ladder for this sort of achievement. There is no formal, worked out, socially accepted system for becoming a higher, self-actualizing, B-valuing person.

It is bad enough that this problem exists, but worse, there is not even a language yet to deal with it meaningfully. The only words that are available for these lofty aspirations (which are embedded very deeply in human nature when our lower needs have been gratified)—which express what Buddhism calls the *Bodhisattvic* (saintly) path—are words with derogatory connotations like "do-gooder," "boy scout," and "bleeding heart." There is simply no way that a young adult today can unabashedly say, "I would like to be a good human being, as good as I can be, and I would like to live a fruitful, useful, and virtuous life." There is no one to speak to such a young person nor even to offer a way to address such sentiments except in the *Being-language* that I use.

Let's be honest: I can hardly offer myself as an example of a typical psychology professor or academician. Certainly, I can advise such youths what to do and where to go, but I am way out on the edge of regular American society. Would any mainstream, vocational-guidance expert or high school counselor offer similar advice? Would even a mainstream psychoanalyst or a psychotherapist tell them anything of the sort?

The American dream must be phrased explicitly. We have much to learn from the anomie of the hippies and of the politically radical Students for a Democratic Society (SDS), and I think that it can all be put down in words and well communicated. For an individual to experience the higher life is certainly possible in the United States, in an affluent society. There's really nothing against such attainment except the ignorance that the higher path exists and these goals are possible to obtain. It is not necessary to develop, as the hippies do, a reaction formation against what they call the "plastic" or materialistic culture—which is all that they know—and then to reject it entirely and to drop out of it.

Foolishly, the hippies are seeking to achieve instantaneously all the noble goals of the *Tzaddik* (Hebrew for saint)—love, lack of domination, community, brotherhood/sisterhood, and the like—immediately and without effort, seemingly just by willing it to be so.

So a paradoxical situation currently exists. The hippie creed does offer the highest values. But these young people don't at all know how to attain these, and so, they end up destroying the very goals for which they wish. Indeed, they find themselves generating the opposite situation of what they are seeking, that is, leading lives of hypocrisy, reaction formation, slovenliness, laziness, mutual exploitation, taking advantage of other people, and just being general nuisances—even though their verbalized values actually are wonderful goals.

The same issue holds true for the politically radical youths who, in effect, want to destroy American society in order to attain these very same goals. However, there is a difference in character structure, I suppose. The SDS types are more active, aggressive, and violent, whereas the hippie types are more passive, receptive, and quiescent. But it should be pointed out that their ultimate goals are identical.

Furthermore, it should be pointed out that these goals are the same goals that all great religions have sought for—as well as the Boy Scouts, the Kiwanis, and virtually every other benevolent organization. All these groups want love, peace, prosperity, social harmony, affection, trust, and the like. I can say it another way: The contemporary anomie in American society—especially of the young—means that they are not feeling loyal to mainstream values but, rather, view them with disgust and horror.

But then I would ask, "What *are* the U.S. values?" I would maintain that these values have not been articulated well and that, consequently, these young adults do not really know what they are. They have historically been phrased only in lower and materialist terms. In other words, there is actually a hierarchy of phrasings of U.S. values, and it seems to be my responsibility to phrase them at their very highest.

After this phrasing is accomplished—and there is a clear depiction of the Jeffersonian dream (which is, after all, truly possible to attain in the United States)—then I must next point out that our society has to legitimize the various professional tracks, educational paths, and vocational ladders to sustain life at these highest levels. This step would require a major revolution in the whole notion of vocational guidance and of personal-educational counseling.

In writing up this conceptualization, I also must be sure to differentiate between the hippies and the SDS youth on one hand—who are the products of affluence and of lower basic-need gratification so that their "grumbles" are actually "higher grumbles"—and the blacks, minority groups, and poor who are at a lower level of grumbles altogether. In the latter case, we could speak about social injustice and feel that there are easily soluble problems to end job discrimination or substandard housing—at least in principle if not in daily political practice. But in the former case, the problems essentially are philosophical, psychological, religious, and theoretical, that is, in terms of the values that people should seek for in everyday life. The former group is seeking for the very highest human values because its lower ones are already satisfied. So, the goals of these two groups are entirely different.

In writing up my analysis, I certainly must make the whole hierarchy of human needs and metaneeds quite explicit. I must say something like this: It is possible in American society to lead a life in which people are not endangered and can feel free of anxiety and fear; in which they can feel intimacy, belongingness, and brotherhood/sisterhood; and in which it is possible and probable that love needs can be satisfied—and that if it is possible to find people to love and to enter into loving relationships, then it is also possible to seek for dignity, pride, and self-respect.

If it is possible to have a society in which these qualities are freely given to everybody as a right, then it is possible to seek for self-actualization and for personal fulfillment of one's personal, unique potentialities and idiosyncrasies. Finally, it is possible to lead a life at the level of beauty, excellence, goodness, truth, perfection, and oneness.

Then, all of these principles can be framed in terms of the following: This is the American dream, or, at least, it *can* be. It certainly should be. That is, it should become a reality, not just remain a dream. This vision ought to be offered to young adults as a real possibility, something that they can choose voluntarily to do and pursue and that, if they work hard enough, they confidently can expect to attain. All the hippie goals actually can be attained; it is just that they are pursuing them in the wrong way. So also for the violent SDS revolutionaries and the black militants: Their goals can be attained, but they are seeking them in the wrong way.

It is important, though, to delineate the differences between protesting the problems of American society in "good faith" versus protesting them in "bad faith." Not only with groups like SDS, the hippies, and black militants is there a major discrepancy between means and ends in their talk. Worse, they frequently seek to disguise their goals of chaos, destruction, and violence by talking about "good ends" or goals. In this sense, they are definitely talking in bad faith.

I think it will help too if even the materialist and money goals of American society are pointed out to be at least *possibly* a good path toward the higher values. That is, wealth and power in the hands of good people are means to good ends. It is just that they are not necessarily so. In the hands of weak, bad, or immature people, money and power can be used for bad purposes, either personally or socially. Thus, part of the total picture should be to work out the reaction formation of many youth today against power and money *at any time and in any hands.*

The fact is that with a lot of money you can buy your way to the Being-values. You can support them, foster them, strengthen them, and the like. There are people in American society—I call them *aggridants*—who do this all the time. I can prove that this phenomenon exists. Money is not necessarily a contaminating thing. Neither are good clothes, fine houses, beautiful gardens, or big cars. These are all means to ends, and in the hands of good people, they are useful and good things.

Another point that Yablonsky (1968) makes is worth quoting:

> The lower-class American delinquent, therefore, is really affirming the validity of the goals of American society by striving for them at any cost. Traditional crime and delinquency in this context is a tribute to the goals and values of American society. The hippie reaction, in contrast, is a condemnation of the total American system. Most youths who drop out into the hippie movement have access to and usually can have all of the cultural prizes of American society. Their condemnation and rejection is total. They reject the American family, religion, education, government, the economic and materialist prizes of American society. More than that, they reject the "game-playing" approach for that acquisition. (p. 318)

But notice how throughout this relevant passage Yablonsky makes no distinction among the different possible phrasings of American values, among the cultural prizes, or among the various goals of American society. Rather, he implies here that, for both the criminals and the hippies, all that the American system has to offer are materialist things. This is simply not true. I think I will go on with this issue later.

I have one last thought in this context. I must speak about the bad job of salesmanship that American culture is doing. That is, the advertising and salesmanship techniques of Madison Avenue and the culture's other sections could very easily be used far better than they have been. Partly, this is a matter of the usual selling-short of human nature in general and of the American character in particular. This situation must be changed.

During the social and political tumult of the late 1960s, Maslow became increasingly interested in relating humanistic psychology to meaningful political theory and action. He was convinced that virtually all politicians and their supporters were basing their positions on obsolete conceptions of human motivation and behavior and that an entirely new politics— rooted in humanistic psychology—was now possible for truly creating a better society. He called this new approach psychopolitics. In this unpublished paper dated July 12, 1969, Maslow set forth some of his thoughts about this intriguing topic.

27

Building a New Politics
Based on Humanistic Psychology

The issue of *countervalues* is an important one. We must discuss the jealousy and envy that many people feel toward the superior, the rich, the powerful, or the beautiful. Because of this same psychological tendency, some individuals today feel this resentful way toward the United States—as though it were a rich uncle or a boss in the workplace. We must expect that almost inevitably, there will be at least some resentment felt toward the lucky or superior individual. Concerning this problem, the psychology of the *aggridant* human being or animal might be conceptually helpful. For instance, the aggridant often adopts various camouflage techniques whereby he or she succeeds in not threatening or debasing the self-esteem of the weaker member of his or her species. In this context, it is also relevant to discuss the *aggridant's noblesse oblige.*

Another major principle in the development of a humanistic psycho-politics is that of universalism or specieshood. Our axiom is that human similarities are deeper than human differences. This general concept in humanistic psychology can become the basis for a universalistic code of values, ethics, and philosophy. In turn, these variables should be able to generate a one-world type of politics—that is, involving complete integration or specieshood. Indeed, I doubt whether a universal politics or world law will ever be possible until we have such a universalistic philosophy. And this philosophy, which I believe is perfectly possible to formulate, must emerge from a universalistic psychology, which already exists in an embryonic form.

It is important to understand that for individuals, cultures, and nations, one should not overvalue safety, security, and belongingness at the *cost* of individual growth toward self-actualization. Any humanistic politics must leave open the path of growth toward self-actualization.

In this light, we can offer the examples of the "freezing" of emotional growth as documented by Zaleznik's (1956, 1966) studies of modern labor unions; that is, for the sake of job security, its members gave up all possibility of personal development. This notion also is relevant for those situations involving inherited special privilege or wealth. For instance, some people who are born into trust funds and the like will devote their lives to protecting their wealth rather than taking chances in growing toward self-actualization. Or, the Mediterranean nations can serve as a good example of the way in which family belongingness and clan loyalty make it almost impossible for any single individual to get very far ahead. In nations like Italy or Spain, one's loyalties and responsibilities toward one's family are often so powerful that one simply does not have adequate time to devote to self-advancement.

Especially at this moment in history, the great problem confronting us is how to maintain a firm social order but still keep open the possibilities toward self-actualization. Certainly, our higher needs and growth possibilities rest squarely on a foundation of safety, solidity, security, or—as the current phrase has it—on "law and order." No real growth is possible without a firm basis of law and order. Yet, it is also possible for a society to become stuck or immobilized at the law-and-order level and to emphasize this condition so much that an individual's possibilities for growth are limited.

Let us be clear. Those who attack our safety needs—our needs for law and order—ultimately are attacking all of our higher needs and *metaneeds* as well. Why? Because political chaos causes people to become more regressed in their underlying motivations. In the midst of a chaotic society, nearly everyone becomes forced to put aside their higher motivations and instead regress toward a seeking of orderliness, stability, legality, and the like. Of course, the big danger then becomes authoritarianism. So, we must always choose between chaos and nihilism on one side and authoritarianism on the other.

But it helps, I think, at least with people of good faith, to stress that safety needs are very deeply rooted in human nature and are *instinctoid* and that we expect these *lower needs* to be prepotent over our higher needs. Therefore, persons of good will certainly will recognize that extremists who are attacking safety, security, and law and order—and who are willing to take a chance on chaos, disorder, and riots for the sake of possible beneficial social or political change—are simultaneously attacking our highest values: beauty, excellence, perfection, and truth.

For this reason, we must say today to advocates for both extremes: "a plague on both your houses." Then, we must try to protect ourselves against our own emotional overreactions, for instance, our very real anger toward those advocating either extreme. The task is to be like a clock in a thunderstorm: just going one's own way without paying any attention to the passing, clamoring noise.

I think it also is vital to discuss the issue of "bad faith." Much political discourse, certainly revolutionary talk, is merely a screen of rationalizations to conceal other, darker motivations that lie hidden from view. Thus, in my own life, I have as a general principle refused to cooperate with a villain—even in a good cause—simply because I mistrust him, and I am apt to regard his embrace of a good cause as simply an excuse. That is to say, he is acting in bad faith.

We also must address the subject of evil. The evil that is generated by a bad social system is not the same as the evil that lies within the human psyche. Good people may be forced to do bad things by an anti*synergic* social order—that is, one that encourages selfishness and discourages mutual helpfulness. Conversely, people who are personally not good-hearted at all may find it to their advantage to behave well, just because their social system is synergic. Actually in the long run, we would be obliged to stress that both aspects would have to be improving simultaneously. That is, we would need to improve the character of our managers and administrators as well as of the larger social system itself. We must better design a society that rewards people for behaving virtuously and makes it disadvantageous for them to behave badly. *We need good people to make a good society, and we need a good society to make good people.* Both tasks must be accomplished simultaneously.

We also can conceptualize three distinct levels of political theorizing. The lowest level is one that I am calling *homeostatic politics.* This is political activity without any great future goals and that simply involves keeping the overall system running adequately on a day-to-day basis. It is political activity geared solely toward keeping the streetcars running and the sewers flowing. One is seeking merely to avoid upset, trouble, or breakdown.

The second level is that of *transition politics.* It is quite different in principle from homeostatic politics because it is very definitely moving toward an ideal goal—which constitutes the third level of politics. That is, with ideal or theoretical, or philosophical or *utopian politics,* we are guided by a goal of a particular kind of good society. Immediately, then, the question arises: How do we change a society that is not all that good into a utopian situation? Transitional politics, therefore, becomes the conscious effort of identifying the principles for living in a "half-good" society and attempting to make it a better one. And these principles can be set forth for all three levels.

Most broadly, how can we define psychopolitics? It is *the deriving from humanistic and transpersonal psychology a viable political philosophy and set of political procedures.* The basic implication is that society is a tool for gratifying human needs and metaneeds. Therefore, we can discuss good politics and bad politics, or good and evil in politics. That which is good helps to gratify human needs and to enhance our growth toward self-actualization. That which is evil does the opposite, or blocks our growth. The best way to conceptualize this outlook is to detail, one by one, the axioms of humanistic psychology and then show what each of these means or implies on the larger, social, and political scene.

It should be noted that so long as national sovereignty exists, there must and will be wars. But in homeostatic politics—involving today the existence of powerful nations—then such a principle as the balance of power is quite sound even though it would be terribly destructive at the level of ideal or utopian politics. The principle of the balance of power provides a way of minimizing wars in a world unfortunately dominated by national sovereignty and in which wars are inevitable. In other words, this particular principle (and many other principles as well) can be understood differently at these three different political levels of discourse or analysis. Indeed, what can be regarded as good at one level can be considered as evil at another.

Another salient point is that in undertaking any major social science program aimed at sociopolitical improvement, we would certainly have to make a major push in broadening our understanding of such intrapsychic qualities as the human propensity for violence, malice, sadism, cruelty, or destructiveness. Of course, we already know a lot about these traits, but the germane facts are scattered throughout six or eight different disciplines. It would require a big team of scholars hunting through all the libraries—that is, through social science knowledge that already exists—to organize this whole subject and provide the answer to a key question for the development of any meaningful psychopolitics: How deeply instinctive is the human tendency toward violence, malice, and evil?

Another point to stress is that any social system, however good or noble its set of laws, ultimately *must* rest on good people. Some of the most inhumane and repressive nations in the world today have, on paper, constitutions and legal systems just as beautiful as those possessed by the most civilized countries. No good social system can just be written down or legislated. Rather, it exists within the people who live it, who carry it out—at every street corner and in every daily activity. If people hate one another, mistrust one another, or try to exploit one another—if they are greedy or malicious—then there is simply no way for setting forth effective laws or rules. It becomes an impossible task. First, the people have to be improved.

It is, therefore, vital to emphasize that a democratic society is rooted in a set of feelings toward other people—feelings like compassion and respect—and that certainly can be integrated with a very realistic understanding of the human capacity for evil. If we did not trust other people, if we did not like them, if we did not pity them, if we did not have brotherly or sisterly feelings for them, then a democratic society would of course be out of the question. Obviously, human history provides many examples to prove this point.

Similarly, for democracy to be effective, it is imperative that individuals be active agents rather than pawns. The whole agent-pawn difference is very basic to formulating a viable system of democratic psychopolitics. As long as most people are conformists in the sense that Solomon Asch's (1965) experimental studies have suggested—or have a low leverage, as in McClelland's (1953, 1961) studies of those with a low need for achievement—then we are faced with a serious question: What proportion of the total population, or how many such pawns, can a society stand without being harmed? We must relate this issue to the research findings concerning the autonomous, or psychologically healthy, person—who is, by definition, an active agent and not a pawn. The psychoanalytic notion of ego strength is also relevant to this discussion.

Finally, I want to make an explicit point about the United States as being the pilot experiment for humanity. We are the ones who are rich, leisured, and lucky. We are the fortunate ones, and we are the only ones who have the time and the will to discuss lofty philosophical principles and to conduct social science experiments. But our experiments must be intended to benefit all humanity, because we are the only ones who can afford to experiment.

In this sense, then, it would be a great step toward universal peace if the United States could again be the hope of the world—as it was in 1900 and 1910—when millions of people throughout the globe wanted to migrate here to achieve a better life. Of course, just to be realistic about it, my belief is that beneath all the seemingly fashionable, anti-U.S. rhetoric promulgated around the world nowadays, this same feeling still holds. That is, if our government totally eliminated all our immigration barriers, virtually everybody in the world would want to live here. And, of course, this reality belies all the "hate America" talk.

A coda to this entire paper is that humanistic psychology, humanistic sociology, humanistic politics, and humanistic philosophy all involve integrations of good and evil. That is, these important approaches must not be understood as seeing only the good within human nature. In this regard, we definitely must develop a humanistic theory of evil—of bad behavior—in order to round out the humanistic psychology that deals with our higher impulses. We understand evil differently when we understand goodness; the two must be conceptually integrated. When they are integrated in this way, they are both different than before this integration took place.

I would emphasize that *Third Force* psychology has certainly pointed out the good possibilities in human nature and that this approach was necessary to counterbalance the extreme pessimism inherent in most traditional religious psychologies and in psychoanalysis. For this reason, many people erroneously have come to assume that humanistic psychology is wholly optimistic and deals only with our highest qualities. But, of course, this assumption is invalid. Our stress on the heights of human nature has simply derived from the necessity for filling in a gap and correcting an overpessimism that reigned too long and too powerfully.

In short, the time has come to integrate our understanding of all aspects of human nature and, in so doing, create a truly comprehensive psychology.

During the late 1960s, Maslow increasingly turned his attention to the relevance of humanistic psychology for effecting meaningful political and social change. In this fragmentary and undated but evocative paper, Maslow offered insights that seem more relevant than ever in a time when many Americans are seeking significant changes in the political process.

28

Further Thoughts
About American Politics

If I still believe in our parliamentary democracy, it is because so far nothing better has offered itself. But I feel strongly that we need to do some hard, realistic thinking about our political system. It is no longer working as it was originally designed to work. Thanks to mass media and the decline of a critical public spirit, our political life is now largely election winning, "image" projecting, public relations, and advertising.

Another weakness of our system as it currently works is that it turns a few hundred men and women into professional politicians, so hard-pressed that they have little time in which to think about anything except politics. The same system leaves all the rest of us shut out of political life and feeling almost helpless in consequence. In England, too much has to happen in Westminster and too little happens elsewhere. For this reason, there is probably a need today for English regional parliaments, if only to relieve the pressure of work in the House of Commons.

The weakness of a completely socialized, collectivist society as exemplified by the Soviet bloc is that it becomes too dependent on central planning

and a slow-moving, unwieldy bureaucracy so that it lacks sufficient enterprise and flexibility. Also, such a society fails to make a real attempt to satisfy
all the consumer needs of its members. But in our own society, most people—especially the young—are subjected to the constant pressures of advertising, sales pitches, and the unscrupulous manipulation of public taste and
spending.

Somewhere between these two extremes, we might be able to create a
society that could combine what is best in both of these divergent systems.
Money would be power under public control, but there also would be plenty
of private enterprise to satisfy the public's lesser needs.

During the last decade of Maslow's life, he became increasingly inter-ested in applying the powerful insights of humanistic psychology to the American workplace. In the 1960s, Maslow's ideas thus came to influence a new generation of managerial theorists and practitioners. In this un-published essay written in June 1969, Maslow as a scholar in residence at the Saga Corporation based in California turned his attention to the role of communication and feedback in the functioning of healthy orga-nizations.

29

Communication

Key to Effective Management

The whole series of recent Saga newspapers forces into my consciousness a new subheading under the *eupsychia* and revolution categories, namely, bigness–smallness. One of the clear issues for the normative social psychologist—and one that I would now add to my article on utopia—is the necessity for integrating the advantages of bigness with those of smallness and for avoiding the disadvantages of bigness and those of smallness. This task can definitely be accomplished—or at least is being attempted—with a fair amount of success, especially in the business world. We have much to learn from this important effort now underway. Perhaps I could take as the simplest model the means by which this issue is being played out in colleges and universities today.

First, there is the phenomenon exemplified by the University of California at Berkeley. This is a huge, monstrous, highly centralized, bureaucratic giant in which feedback and customer satisfaction have been nearly entirely lost. Communication occurs only downward—from a handful of top administrators to thousands of students and faculty—and never effectively upward. Such a huge, impersonal, and bureaucratic organization almost inevitably engenders feelings of helplessness, of not being heard, of having no control over one's fate, and of being a pawn rather than an agent. The same situation was true at Columbia University, where a major student rebellion occurred. Perhaps it was even worse there as its president, trustees, administrators in general, and faculty lacked the slightest idea of what was occurring among its customers—that is, its student population.

On the national political level, we can take the governments of France and the Soviet Union as examples of bureaucratic monstrosity. In both countries, there has been a nearly total centralization of power, with all sorts of consequent inefficiencies and stupidities leading to feelings of helplessness and rage among its citizens. Here again, the missing element has been the presence of meaningful communication upward—that is, feedback from customers. There has been almost no attention paid to customer satisfaction or wishes.

It is interesting to me that in both countries, the dominant system has broken down completely after *never* working well. What is now being instituted in replacement is almost inevitably a system of greater communication upward, more local control, and more decentralization and meaningful planning only after receiving feedback from customers. I think this whole approach can be summarized aptly by one phrase: *individual self-choice.*

An important issue for managers is to retain the advantage of smallness so that the individual is given a choice among alternatives and then is encouraged to express his or her preference by the act of purchasing, registering in a particular course or college, or "voting" with one's feet by migrating to another place, and the like. I hadn't realized it fully before, but the whole of the democratic managerial approach—whether we call it *Theory Y management* or *enlightened management*—can be seen from the viewpoint of essentially participatory, localized, decentralized democracy, with consequently excellent customer feedback and with control being exerted at the individual, personal, and grassroots level.

The present issue of the Saga newspaper has an interesting article on the use of surveys in management. It provides me with an excellent example from which I can leap into conceptual generalizations about management, politics, democracy, and societal improvement. That is, the key aspect of Saga's own corporate history is that from the very beginning—when initiating food service at Hobart College back in 1948—Saga circulated surveys among students to obtain their reactions. This informal method of word-of-mouth, face-to-face evaluation has continued, but it also has been expanded to a larger, more conscious, efficient, and computerized system.

However, it is vital to emphasize that, at bottom, this approach is a matter of *attitude*. An authoritarian person or organization does not ask, listen, or solicit honest feedback. Rather, it tells, orders, or makes pronouncements, without obtaining feedback, evaluation, or assessing customer satisfaction or gaining any real knowledge of how the system is actually working. In contrast, the democratic attitude, which arises from a person's character structure and from societal arrangements, involves a profound respect for other people. I might even describe this attitude as one of compassion, agapean love, or openness to others: a willingness—even an eagerness—to listen. The final consequences of this attitude necessitate a presenting to others of opportunities for true self-choice among real alternatives.

So, if you like human beings; if you like to see them grow; if you think they have a higher nature that can be cultivated; if you experience real satisfaction from the growth, happiness, and self-actualization of other people; if you enjoy their pleasure; if you feel brotherly or sisterly toward them and share their realm of discourse, then you will almost inevitably create certain kinds of social organizations or systems. In contrast, authoritarian "bosses" reject any sense of kinship with the "bossed," with pawns, and with their supposed inferiors.

Another element in the vocabulary for this democratic attitude is *Taoistic respect*. It again arises not from shaping, manipulating, bossing, or controlling other persons but, rather, from respecting them enough to allow and encourage them to affirm their own tastes, preferences, and choices. Taoistic respect in management also involves an active effort to respond to all feedback by improving the alternatives from which self-choice is made.

This idea also can be discussed from the viewpoint of pragmatic consequences (validation, assessment, evaluation, and noting how something works). In private industry, a very efficient form of feedback has come into existence with aspects like profit-and-loss statements, inventory statements, production quantity and quality statements, and the like. All of these constitute a very quick method of cybernetic-like feedback that tells how well the system is functioning and how efficiently it is being run. Of course, when one has such knowledge, then one is armed against catastrophe and break-down. For example, if there is a red warning light in one part of the system, that indicates there is trouble and then one can immediately go to that part of the system to correct and improve it. However, if there is no such feedback mechanism, then any difficulty in any one part of the system remains as it is—to perhaps cure itself but, more likely, to worsen until the total system breaks down.

Also involved here is the general question of the "wisdom of the body"—a theory that presupposes the value of self-choice. Here we can cite all the physiological research, such as dealing with food preferences, but, in addi-tion, my own studies on college students' evaluations of their professors' knowledge and competency. For example, I discovered that the students' judgments were just as accurate as those of the professors' own colleagues—a finding that indicated a great deal more student "wisdom" than was gener-ally acknowledged at the time. There is a lot of such data from a variety of subfields in psychology that could be synthesized. Indeed, I believe that it would be useful in the larger strategy of developing a humanistic ethic in social science and management to produce a summary article on all the data on the wisdom, or lack of wisdom, of individual self-choice.

It seems that the core of my outlook—at least so far as humanistic man-agement or politics is concerned—is the notion that everything springs from the individual's own character structure, that is, whether it is essentially democratic or authoritarian. It is also my firm conviction that the humanistic approach really does make people feel happier and more fulfilled, in effect, in being heard and understood and in leading active lives rather than existing like helpless pawns. To feel oneself an agent is precisely the opposite from feeling controlled, shoved around, dominated, and the like.

An authoritarian individual or system produces these latter effects on others. A democratic individual or system produces the former effects. It is, therefore, no surprise that given a choice, almost everyone will choose the democratic individual, organization, and society. For to do so is certainly to side with personal pleasure and happiness. We also can add from the view-point of self-development that the democratic, compassionate, loving, re-specting, and growth-enjoying attitude in the stronger person leads to growth and self-fulfillment in the weaker. In other words, the basic premises of humanistic psychology form the foundation for enlightened management, politics, and social change.

Finally, returning to the theme of the necessity for integrating bigness-smallness, I think it is useful to point out that the problem does not even arise in the small, personal, face-to-face enterprise, school, or social situation. It is only when a successful, one-person business starts becoming much bigger that these problems come up. If we are conscious of the advantages of small-ness and customer satisfaction—and have knowledge of what is occurring generally—then we can be forewarned and can arrange to grow larger, as Saga executives have effectively done with their company.

We can institutionalize all the democratic, communicative, respecting, loving, listening, customer-satisfaction kinds of things by using the advan-tages of technology, in other words, keeping all the benefits of smallness but also capitalizing on the benefits of bigness.

For instance, several articles in this same issue of *Tempo* show the advan-tages of mass-marketing, mass-purchasing, the division of labor, and being able to hire specialized experts of various kinds in order to improve on what the smaller, face-to-face enterprise does unconsciously and intuitively.

What shall I call this revolutionary new approach? Theory Y manage-ment? Enlightened management? *Humanistic management?* Perhaps the lat-ter is the most worthwhile term, because it implies real respect, liking, and understanding of humankind's higher possibilities.

I wish to offer one little addition. The whole system of feedback works best if customers are able to express their opinions—that is, their dis-approval, anger, or enthusiasm—immediately. Continuous and instantaneous feedback seems to be the ideal. I have heard that this method has been in-stituted by Hollywood film companies, in which viewers push "feedback buttons" at the very moment that they are witnessing a particular scene on screen. The more we can emulate such an approach throughout management today, the better our society will become.

By the mid-1960s, Maslow had become thoroughly disenchanted with the dominant values and worldview of most intellectuals within the United States. Slowly moving toward a stance that today would be most closely linked to neoconservatism, Maslow felt sure that the failure of most liberal intellectuals to recognize the reality of human evil had serious social and political consequences. In this unpublished essay written in January 1967, Maslow addressed the issue.

30

See No Evil, Hear No Evil

When Liberalism Fails

It seems time to address a major flaw of contemporary liberalism. First of all, we can recognize that the liberals (who are generally intellectually and aesthetically oriented and physically ectomorphic) do not really have a good theory or experiential recognition of the existence of evil, either in themselves or in others. Nor do liberals possess an adequate theory or experiential recognition of the drive for power in themselves or in others.

We could almost define contemporary liberals in terms of precisely this crucial issue: They assume that people are not evil and that they are uninterested in power, never struggle for it, and always use it wisely. From this central, liberal axiom, all sorts of hidden, covert, unconscious implications and deductions arise about fighting criminals, or the Mafia, or the Las Vegas gang, or ruthless figures like the Teamster gangster-boss Jimmy Hoffa. Significantly, he never claimed innocence of the federal government's charges

160

against him but only protested that it had not behaved in the correct, liberal fashion.

To put it another way, it is as if the liberals thought that the "rules of the game"—such as concerning the nature of admissible legal evidence, protection of individual privacy, and the Bill of Rights—were somehow autonomous. They forget what the rules of the game were designed *for*—that is, what the goals of law and constitutions and so on are supposed to be about.

In many Western countries, liberals unfortunately today are perfectly willing to see the ultimate goals and ends of a society—that is, justice, truth, order, law, safety, security, virtue, and so on—let go and dissolve just as long as parliamentary rules of procedure and orderliness are observed. In the strictest sense that psychiatrist Eric Berne has used the term, liberals view our society's institutions as only a *game* rather than as vital, instrumental activities for realizing authentic values and goals.

In this context, we would certainly have to discuss the new drug rehabilitation program called Synanon. It seems to work very well in rehabilitating people like heroin addicts and convicted felons who are emotionally completely broken down. It must be fully accepted that Synanon at the very outset is geared to imposing a completely strong, authoritarian, dictatorial, and harsh hand—a set of rules deliberately intended to break the will, pride, and arrogant self-image of drug addicts—by forcing them to the "bottom of the barrel" and making them accept humility, weakness, helplessness, and defeat—essentially, by treating them from the outset as would a very stern father.

The parallels for the law in our society are obvious. After all, the purpose of law is to advance people toward justice and the other *Being-values,* not merely to enable them to play the game well. For those who are diminished human beings, who are living at the lowest motivational levels, who are blatantly immature in just about the same sense as a 4-year-old child—their pressing, primary need, before any rehabilitation and inner maturation can take place, is the stern and forceful father, the clear and irrevocable rule, the absolutely unclouded relationship between these rules and the Being-values and the ultimate goals.

The same principle seems just as true—perhaps, even more so—for so-called underdeveloped countries, that is, those nations, cultures, or communities that function at this same low motivational level or that live in an immature and childish way. Such countries also require a stern, strong hand. All the data and theories that we have about human motivation point in this direction. And yet, it would be virtually impossible to convince contemporary liberals to agree with this viewpoint. Instead, they foolishly insist on treating diminished human beings in precisely the same manner as those who are highly mature and responsible. Liberals persist in treating psychopaths, paranoids, and schizophrenics in the same way as though they were self-actualizing people. Why is this so? A psychologically based explanation seems necessary.

SLAVE MORALITY

Could it be that being physically weak (ectomorphic, intellectual, and aesthetic), the characteristic liberal feels a form of Nietzschean resentment or *slave morality?* By this term, I am referring to the morality of the weak in the face of the strong whom they fear and envy in an impotent way. Because our society's intellectuals write the laws and institute the rules of the game, how much of such misguided behavior ultimately originates in the weaklings' fear of the strong *aggridant?* Of the muscular mesomorph? The curious thing is that as psychologist William Sheldon has shown, our society's criminals and delinquents—especially the gang leaders—usually are recruited from the ranks of the mesomorphs. These people are precisely the kind who would be leaders at anything they set out to accomplish. If they weren't gang leaders, they would be corporate presidents or senators.

Mesomorphs simply are apt to play a different game and by different rules. They are apt to take what they want and to believe unconsciously that essentially justice consists of the strong person's winning the spoils of war— riches, women, and so on—and that this outcome is appropriate, equitable, fair, and just. Such people are less likely to resent in the Nietzschean way of impotent envy. Instead, they are more apt to resent in open hostility toward the dominant hierarchy; that is, they are ready to fight and will feel angry if beaten. Also, their aggressive, emotional stance is probably more likely to be *conscious*—"They'll be sorry they ever tangled with me!"—rather than unconscious in the form of depression, as we might typically expect with the weaker, nonaggridant.

Perhaps we could phrase matters in this way: The ectomorph lives by one set of rules and for one set of purposes, whereas the mesomorph lives by a completely different set of rules and for different purposes. Certainly, the mesomorph is more likely to be interested in power, material wealth, possession of objects, gaining sexual partners as conquests, and generally being "King-of-the-hill." In the muscularly weak ectomorph, the drive to dominance is typically muted and may go underground altogether. In any case, if the ectomorph is indeed to become king-of-the-hill, it must be through aesthetic and intellectual means and definitely not through muscular struggle, open fighting, physical violence, or warfare.

Perhaps this explanation is why ectomorphic liberals have developed their seemingly self-defeating set of rules, which would probably be suitable for governing a society of other ectomorphs and intellectuals—but which are obviously so unsuited for fighting aggridant criminals and lawbreakers, mesomorphs, and physically strong people.

Certainly, my analysis holds true on the international scene as well. Not only in this country but also throughout the West, when liberals are discussing the Vietnam War, they are far more apt to criticize the United States for small sins as well as big ones, to distort evidence, to tell lies, and to be unscrupulous. Liberals are more apt to be perfectionistic in demanding that the United States behave officially in a saintly fashion but being wholly willing to accept without a word of protest whatsoever horrible crimes and evils that the Communists are apt to perpetrate.

For instance, the Society for Psychologists Concerned With Social Issues (SPSSI) recently passed a resolution—the first of its kind in the organization's history—condemning the torture of North Vietnamese prisoners by the South Vietnamese and then blaming such conduct on the U.S. intervention in Indochina. But not one word was uttered in this resolution about the fact that all Vietnamese routinely torture and kill their prisoners of war and that the North Vietnamese government has instituted an official policy of authorizing assassination, murder, and terrorism. The Vietcong have killed by terrorism many more Vietnamese than Americans have killed even with all their technologically sophisticated weaponry of war. And yet, the SPSSI selected only the United States to criticize.

This activity is akin to the spirit with which the English philosopher Bertrand Russell—the perfect ectomorph who is thin, physically weak, intellectual, and a priori in his reasoning—blamed the Indochinese slaughter of the Communists and everybody else in sight on the United States, though our country was not even on the scene. Again, the classic liberal has selected without batting an eyelash the most just and fair nation to attack yet all the while accepting the overt and frank evil of authoritarian people and regimes.

This outlook parallels the liberals' insistence that our government be absolutely perfect and pure—and simply allow organized criminals like the Mafia and Murder, Inc. to play by a completely different set of rules involving bribery, threats, intimidation, and outright violence. It is clear that liberals never seem to get angry at Jimmy Hoffa or the Mafia. It is as if liberals have accepted the evil of evil people and have ceased to fight it anymore but keep on demanding perfection and saintliness in themselves and in our government, laws, judges, and courts.

Another source of ultimate psychodynamic explanation may arise from what I have observed about mesomorphic- or aggridant-fighters for power. That is, such people have a tendency to live by a set of mesomorphic rules, as if these composed a code of ethics. This code tacitly affirms the "right" of the strong to fleece and to dominate the weak, timid, or naive. It is as if mesomorphs deep down, unconsciously feel that the weak and timid have no right to protest or fight back. Certainly, mesomorphs become surprised when the weakling does retaliate.

But furthermore, it is my impression—though I certainly cannot prove it—that not only do mesomorphs become surprised but they also become indignant about the lamblike person who suddenly turns and tenaciously fights back like a wolf. For the mesomorph, the lamb should *remain* a lamb and always act like one—not abruptly turn around and bite, scratch, and retaliate. The mesomorph is apt to feel a kind of good-natured contempt for the timid and weak one, perhaps even to take care of him as well as to exploit, dominate, step on, and use him. But this good-natured contempt is present only so long as the weak one knows his place!

A good example of this principle can be seen in the way that southern whites treated black people 40 or 50 years ago in the United States. In a certain sense, the whites "took care of," helped, and protected the blacks but only so long as black people accepted their part in the equation—the notion that they were not quite human and, therefore, did not deserve full civil and human rights. In the South, therefore, two classes of humankind existed, and this, in turn, led to the establishment of two different sets of laws, rules, ethics, and values. It is something like this phenomenon that I vaguely see in the relationship between the strong and weak, the predatory and prey, the aggridant and the *schlemiel* (Yiddish for bumbling fool).

SOCIAL IMPLICATIONS

This entire subject will have to be discussed in my course on utopia and, ultimately, in any wider system of social psychology and in any comprehensive theory of evolution toward the better society. Long ago, it became clear to me that no society can function very successfully—especially not in a world of separate, sovereign nation-states—unless there is a built-in arrangement whereby the aggridants, innovators, geniuses, and trailblazers of all types and in all fields are admired and valued and are not torn apart by those seething with Nietzschean resentment, impotent envy, and weakling *countervaluing.*

Thus far, the only preventive strategy that I have been able to suggest is that society's leaders, strong ones, high achievers, and winners receive their pay in relation to higher needs and *metaneed* gratifications rather than in the obvious, *lower-need* gratifications like money and material wealth.

For example, such persons might become like the Grey Eminence and wear monks' robes—taking vows of poverty—and enjoy less wealth, collectible objects, and material affluence than the average members of the society. That is, aggridant leaders probably are quite happy anyway with the simple life so long as their higher needs and metaneed gratifications are available and especially the idiosyncratic satisfactions of actualizing their unique selfhood. The freedom to do what one wishes, to get things done, to improve things without hindrance and without having to convince a lot of people or seduce them into supporting it—this kind of thing would constitute the highest possible reward for aggridants, leaders, winners, and trailblazers.

In this envisioned system, average people might actually be paid *more* in dollars, appliances, automobiles, and so on and, therefore, not have to feel envious, resentful, or jealous of society's leaders. So far as I can conceive, this arrangement should work out rather well. I might extend this principle to say that it is a good idea to pay people with goods and services valuable for themselves but not for others.

For instance, suppose we could pay mesomorphs with mesomorphic treasures like the opportunity to engage in the most attractive, appealing forms of mountain climbing, surfboarding, deep-sea diving, or football playing. Certainly, these are activities that hold little appeal for ectomorphs or that might even repulse them. For this reason, such pay would arouse minimal envy for ectomorphs. Meanwhile, they would be paid in terms of ready access to books and manuscripts, fine libraries, classical musical concerts, and the like—rewards that hold virtually no appeal for mesomorphs. In this manner, everybody would be happy. This situation would resemble the ideal marriage in which each partner receives unique satisfactions from the relationship and neither envies the other.

Ultimately, such theorizing for the entire society—and at the larger, political level of national sovereignty—has to accept the reality that strong leadership is always necessary for underdeveloped or primitive societies today. Of course, the great problem throughout human history has been that such strong figures are likely to be evil, if not at the outset, then due to the seemingly inevitable, corrupting effects of exerting power over others. So far as I can determine, this problem can never be solved in *principle* within the system of national sovereignty itself. It must have some international sanction. There must be some supernational power that can enforce its rule over a national, authoritarian boss like a Hitler or a Stalin. Also, there would have to be some way of making this superentity's stern, fatherly hand a temporary, transitional state of affairs while people were being educated and brought up to more mature levels, until finally the society could govern itself by a political democracy and ultimately even by philosophical anarchism and decentralization.

I will have to attempt the development of a set of rules or laws that could apply to both the strong and weak simultaneously. Yet, is this really possible? Perhaps the ultimate development of a psychological theory of power or evil would discover ways of solving these sorts of dilemmas. Perhaps, after all, it will turn out 50 years from now that it would indeed be possible to have different sets of laws for different kinds of people, just as we do for children and adults. Perhaps we will have different sets of laws for strong leaders and weak followers, or for mesomorphs, ectomorphs, and endomorphs.

Also, we will have to resolve the paradoxes that are inherent in the legal, police, and power relationships that exist between the normal citizenry that lives by metarules and metalaws—that is, at a very high level of maturity—and the criminal population, which lives by a low set of rules, that is, of "punching below the belt," "stabbing in the back," "shooting from behind," assassinating one's opponents, and the like. Clearly, it is possible for a whole society to be taken over and ruled by criminals, as has happened in Sicily, Batista's Cuba, "Papa Doc" Duvalier's Haiti, and dozens of other countries in Africa, Latin America, and elsewhere. The only way of eliminating the Mafia in Sicily and, for that matter, in Las Vegas—as nearly as I can determine—would be to abandon the high rules and efficiently pick up the low rules once the criminals have demonstrated that they want to play that way.

It is perfectly silly to wrestle with someone bent on injury or murder while you are shackling or handcuffing yourself. It is obviously silly for a whole culture to allow itself to be destroyed by adhering to the rules of a genteel game like tennis while one's opponents are playing a brutally different game and by a brutally different set of rules. Society is not a game; it is a serious life-or-death effort. Rules are just means, instruments, and techniques. They have absolutely no meaning in themselves. Rather, their meaning lies entirely in the ultimate goals and ends for which they serve. When societal rules start to develop a functional autonomy, that can become a very sick or dangerous thing for everyone.

And, it looks as if something of the sort is starting to happen with power libertarians and with self-hating Americans today, not to mention such anti-American foreigners as the French who support Charles de Gaulle. Concerning the French and their anti-Americanism, the issue is probably a simple matter of Nietzschean resentment, impotent envy, and hatred because of past favors done for its citizenry. In this context, it is useful to recall the witty, incisive statement attributed to the English playwright George Bernard Shaw: "I don't know why he should hate me. I never did anything nice for him."

꧁ While teaching at Brooklyn College in the late 1930s, Maslow was a supporter of President Franklin D. Roosevelt's democratic New Deal program. As a result, Maslow often found himself condemned as a fascist by more radical Stalinist and Trotskyite faculty members active on campus. In this unpublished and undated article written between 1938 and 1941, Maslow offered his perspective on a personality type he was frequently encountering in the politically heated years of the late Depression. The paper is also historically significant, because it predated by several years the landmark personality study titled The Authoritarian Personality *(Adorno, Frenkel-Brunswick, Levinson, & Sanford, 1950) published after World War II and to which Maslow conceptually contributed.*

31

The Communist Personality

The following is an extemporaneous statement that really expresses my memory or my general impression of data that I have accumulated. I have not performed a careful analysis of such data, and therefore, in the absence of further proof, my remarks are to be taken as tentative.

In brief, my strong impression is that it is possible to evaluate the Communists with whom I have worked clinically on a personality continuum of emotional security versus insecurity. However, this continuum probably does not form a normal, bell-shaped curve distribution. Rather, the distribution seems to tend toward bimodality, that is, with large clusters manifesting on the continuum's two ends or extremes. In this sense, my remarks are typological in focus.

To offer a crude estimate, about 90% of the approximately 30 Communists with whom I have worked clinically have been quite emotionally insecure in character type. A fair proportion of these people have even been neurotic, sometimes overtly manifesting—and sometimes not—frank neurotic symptoms. Such character types can be summarized briefly as follows: *These are frustrated, embittered, and hostile people.* They typically have led miserable lives in which the main etiological factor of interest to us has been the experience of personal rejection, both by their parents and the wider social environment.

It may be clinically said of such persons that they were cases of love starvation. Generally, this primary, insecurity-producing stimulus has been reinforced by other originators of emotional insecurity—such as poverty, unemployment, religious prejudice, and harsh competition—although this latter cluster of factors is not necessarily always present.

More specifically, the general characteristics of this Communist personality type involve the following traits: (a) deeply embedded suspicion and mistrust of others; (b) feelings of conflict and frustration; (c) general pessimism, particularly with respect to the capabilities of other human beings; (d) general anxiety; (e) strong impulses for hostility; (f) various disturbances of self-esteem that are too complex to be summarized here; and, perhaps most important, (g) various disturbances concerning the expression of power.

Regarding this last point, it may be fairly said that their unconscious material shows strong impulses for domination and for revenge and an unconscious acceptance of the worldview that sees all social relations in terms of an underdog-overdog dichotomy. In addition, these individuals typically wish to change their own self-perceived status from underdog to overdog.

Such persons are Communists for a multiplicity of motivations, some good and some bad. The good motivations usually are intellectual and in some, though certainly not all, cases are clearly rationalizations. These are the Communists who will probably cease to be Communists as soon as their own personal conflicts are assuaged and their own personal frustrations satisfied. If I were the leader of a Communist organization, I would not want such people as members, because a large proportion of them will undoubtedly drop away once they obtain a good job, make a good marriage, and the like.

In general, such people make no real effort to understand the opposition, because their unconscious motivation is not to analyze or even to convert but rather *to hate and to feel superior to.* Their usual technique of trying to

convert other persons to Communism will certainly prove ineffective because it consists essentially of sneering, derogating, or forcing. In a word, it
may be said that their character structure will tend to compel them, even
when they are proselytizing, to spit in the eye of the would-be convert.
Among such Communists, I often find no essential love for humanity but
rather the opposite.

At the other end of the continuum, we find individuals who are so completely different that it almost seems foolish to group them together by the
same political label. My guess is that this latter group constitutes perhaps
5% or 10% of the total number of Communists but that they are important
beyond their relatively small numbers.

This group comprises people who are essentially secure in their basic
character structure even if they have sometimes shown superficial symptoms
of insecurity. Their primary characteristic is that they really love other human
beings, both individually and in the mass; secondly, they have a perception
of other human beings as essentially good, lovable, and trustworthy. This
latter outlook is what I call general optimism.

Out of the deeply embedded social interest of such individuals—that is,
their love for humanity at large and for their neighbors in particular—they
will inevitably try to improve humanity's lot. For instance, instead of merely
speaking platitudes, such persons will actually be kind, sympathetic, helpful,
and altruistic to their neighbors, family members, or subordinates in the
workplace. The essential thing about such persons is that *they are deeply hurt
by injustice, cruelty, unfairness, exploitation, and unhappiness even when
they are not directly involved.*

Etiologically, many of these people as children did not suffer from rejection or frustration, and in any case, none of them either consciously or unconsciously presently experiences a sense of rejection. Their beliefs about
Communism and world improvement arise not from their own misery but
from other sources. That is, they may be either wealthy or poor, employed
or unemployed, treated well or treated badly by their social environment—
and still, it may be expected that their sentiments will remain constant so
long as their character does not change because of their external influences.
Practically speaking, this means that they may be expected to remain Communists even if they fare well in the world.

It is typical of such Communists that they try very hard to understand their
opposition and often may unconsciously sympathize with it. For instance,
their interpretation of Marxism tends to take the form that the capitalist is

not essentially a bad person but is forced to behave badly because of external forces that make him into an exploiter. Thus, it is possible for such Communists to be friends with people who do not believe as they do.

People who have this character structure are always world-improvers as soon as there are various ways by which the world may be improved. Of course, not all such persons are Communists. Rather, the contrary is true. My impression from my study of emotionally secure characters is that generally they will tend *not* to become Communists for various, external reasons that have little to do with disagreement about fundamental Marxist theory. That is, they might ordinarily prefer a type of socialistic, internationally minded world, but they disagree with the particular tactics of the Communist Party— or, as is common, dislike very much the individuals who are actually Communists. Or, they may not like the hierarchical structure of the Communist Party or the way it has developed in Russia today.

Furthermore, it is my impression that if they are Communists, these types of people often tend to be unhappy about the actual tactics of the Communist Party and may sometimes have to force themselves to be loyal to it.

32

Leaders, Pawns, and Power

A Letter to Henry Geiger

Dear Henry:
Last night, I was suffering again from insomnia. I was struggling with all my seemingly contradictory conclusions about self, identity, and intra-psychic concerns on the one hand and social, organizational, and political matters on the other hand. It is rather clear to me now that for individualist psychology, "time wounds all heels" and that virtue pays more often than not. I think that I could prove this hypothesis to be true by using not only clinical material but also orthodox research data as well.

Essentially, I have concluded that over the course of a lifetime—in the proverbial long run—the probability is approximately five to one that evil will be punished. That virtue also will be rewarded seems to have a probability of only about six to five, but it is nevertheless greater than mere chance.

Yet, the really key issue is that punishment and reward are largely intrapsychic, that is, relating to one's sense of happiness, peacefulness, and serenity and to the absence of negative emotions like regret, remorse, or guilt. So as far as external rewards are concerned, these are apt to come in terms of basic-need gratification for belongingness, feeling loved and respected, and generally inhabiting a more platonic world of pure beauty, truth, and virtue. That is, our rewards in life are *not* necessarily apt to be in terms of money, power, or social status of the ordinary sort. Thus, we need to more precisely define what we mean by such words as "reward" and "punishment."

In order to sustain a relatively good society, or relatively adequate level of affluence, it definitely seems important that most persons believe in a just outcome regarding reward and punishment for individual behavior. But even for our present society at this time, I believe I could prove my point that evil people are punished in the intrapsychic ways I have suggested above and that good persons get rewarded (although with a much lower probability) in the same ways.

UNDERSTANDING POWER-SEEKERS

Now what has been troubling me as I have been doing exploratory research—that is, "poking" around and thinking continuously—is the matter of power. I am referring specifically to strong and tough persons, those who are power-seekers and power-wielders. These people can be either good or evil, but it is my impression that the very attainment of power tends to tip most individuals over toward becoming evil rather than good. This situation poses a great mystery, and I have no idea why it is so, beyond offering a few unverified guesses. It is certainly true that, in some instances, greater status or power actually ennobles people and makes them live up to their new role or opportunity. The classic example is Harry Truman, who as president of the United States accomplished much more than anyone had expected.

In any case, it definitely seems that power-seekers—who are somewhat more apt to become evil than good—show a tendency to advance upward in the social order and actually attain power. In this context, I remember an old novel titled *The Blood of the Conquerors,* written by Harvey Fergusson (1921/1971). The story recounts how a Mexican American in a small new Mexican town is pitted politically against a hard-bitten "Yankee." The Yankee is an obsessional and relentless power-seeker, subordinating everything in life to its attainment.

Therefore, he finally triumphs over the Mexican, who occasionally stops from the political battle to "smell the daisies" and enjoy the sunshine.

This dichotomy seems to differentiate the truly powerful American figures like John F. Kennedy and Lyndon B. Johnson from those like Adlai Stevenson, who really did not seem to possess the same drive—or personal need—for taking over the reins of government. From the gossip we hear about Stevenson, he insisted on enjoying a good life personally. And of course, to do so takes time and energy away from the relentless pursuit of political power.

Therefore, personages like Stevenson, or even Abraham Lincoln and Thomas Jefferson, are at a disadvantage in the long run in their relationship to those who are ruled by an indomitable drive for power. When these more "benign" figures do achieve power, it is generally because they have been chosen by others and accepted the responsibilities or because they have walked into the power struggle and consciously played the game by its conventional, "no-holds-barred" rules.

Parenthetically, it is precisely this issue that has reconciled me to the necessity for individual mortality. That is, suppose we doubled our present life span. Then, most likely, more of these power-seekers would remain in control of the world for much longer periods of time. For example, Abram Sachar—our president at Brandeis University—is a power-needer and power-seeker. Because of his advancing chronological age, he probably has only another 4, 5, or 10 years to live, and this is a good thing. Like Napoleon, Lyndon B. Johnson, and similar power-persons, Sachar at one point was absolutely necessary—that is, for the original task of building this private university. It was a one-man job, and Sachar performed it beautifully and efficiently. It is quite clear that such a miracle could not have taken place without such a power-wielder at the helm.

But now that the building phase has been completed, what the university requires is a governor—or let's rather say, an "older brother," or a first among equals. We no longer need a dominating, authoritarian boss with all the power in his own hands. Undoubtedly, our next president at Brandeis University will be a milder, more brotherly, and more affectionate man than Sachar. But suppose people like him lived to be 150 years old? What would happen to this educational institution and other social institutions? If it weren't for human mortality, these people would literally control the world.

THE WEAK SELF

Another matter recently became clear to me while I was doing managerial consulting in California: Most people lack a strong sense of self. They do not know what they want or what they are looking for in life. As a result, they are extremely suggestible and will follow a self-confident leader rather than determine their own destinies.

Now, one key aspect about leadership is that effective leaders are unequivocally decisive. They do not exhibit uncertainty, ambivalence, inner conflict, or ambiguity. In essence, they hide their uncertainties and keep them securely contained. The ocean liner captain cannot afford to be a vacillating Hamlet but must always appear strong.

Well, if we accept as a statistical fact that the average American citizen will do whatever the salesperson suggests or will follow a strong leader rather than a thoughtful, complicated one, then another element enters in the subject of leadership: decisiveness. What do I mean? Namely, that there is no more decisive-looking person in the world than a paranoid character. Also, there is no power-seeker more stubborn and persistent than the one who is paranoid. Such persons never relent for a moment. They never stop to laugh, joke, or enjoy the flowers but just press on persistently.

Now for me, this reality offers a solution—or at least a partial solution—to the terribly depressing historical fact that frequently the political leaders who have led the modern world into disaster have been paranoid characters: Hitler, Stalin, and probably Mao Tse-tung as well. In the United States, Senator Joseph McCarthy and Robert Welch (head of the ultraconservative John Birch Society) also have shown this trait. If we examine the annals of political leadership, we often learn that such personages have been paranoid, but unfortunately, we acquire such knowledge only after the damage has already been done. But then the horrifying question arises: Why do such emotionally disturbed people so frequently find it easy to win loyal followers who are thereon led to destruction?

I remember wondering particularly about the right-wing John Birch Society in southern California and came to the same conclusion as Dostoyevsky, Erich Fromm, and other thinkers that many people are afraid of freedom and would prefer to have their decisions made for them.

Long ago, my wife, Bertha, was working as a salesperson in a New York City department store. She was shocked to discover that most of the customers had no idea what they wanted to buy and were requesting almost pathetically to be told. This situation occurred in the gift department, where personal aesthetic taste was important. But in a dismaying percentage of people, this aesthetic sense was utterly lacking. Bertha concluded that it would be possible to sell *anything* at all simply by making a sales pitch. Of course, she never attempted to do so and finally quit the job out of horror for the whole business. But the other salespersons did, as a matter of course, "push" whatever product they needed to dispose of and were generally quite successful at it.

If this phenomenon exists, then it becomes understandable that most people are seeking leaders. And if they are seeking leaders who must appear strong, self-confident, and unshakable, then we can better comprehend why they should flock after paranoid or selfish power-seekers or those who just *have* to control everybody and everything. We also can understand why more thoughtful, rational people—who can see both sides of an issue—would not appeal very much to those seeking absolute decisiveness. Finally, because selfish, narcissistic, and power-driven people find it easier to use others as mere tools for self-advancement, it makes sense why they disproportionally gain power.

In short, I have been developing some explanations for bridging the gap regarding the matter of virtue's rewards in the intrapsychic world and the choices of vicious people in the social, public, and interpersonal world.

AFTER SELF-ACTUALIZATION, WHAT?

In the intrapsychic realm, the first great task is to search for one's identity. Each person must find his or her true, active self, and after that task is accomplished, then life's real problems lie ahead. Clearly, this task is related to finding one's vocation, or calling, or biological destiny. That is, what is the mission that one chooses to love and sacrifice to?

It is as if we had two kinds of intrapsychic psychologies: one involving our daily struggle toward self-actualization and the other involving a completely different psychology or set of rules for living the clean, pure existence of the mystic or sage.

These rules are quite different in various, surprising ways. For instance, there are conventional, classic sorts of research design emphasizing statistics. My graduate students are apt to regard me as inconsistent or even hypocritical when I stress that they must acquire such tools. But now, I have learned to explain that what I am against is the obsessional use of so-called objective tests and statistics *instead* of being guided by one's inner intuitions. I can say that the person who has acquired a sense of self, direction, and vocation can use all of these tools simply as tools. The tools serve rather than boss their user.

For instance, one of my most talented graduate students is completing her dissertation on *peak-experiences* during natural childbirth. She has made many wonderful discoveries but first had to learn data entry, statistical analysis, and the like. It was all for a very good cause. The IBM computer has definitely been her servant and not her boss. In no sense does it rule her. She is now a good person but with stronger muscles.

That is the key point: First you must be a good person and have a strong sense of selfhood and identity. Then immediately, all the forces in the world become tools for one's own purposes. At once, they cease to be forces that cause, determine, and shape but become instruments for the self to use as it wishes. The same principle is true for money. In the hands of a strong and good person, money is a great blessing. But in the hands of weak or immature persons, money is a terrible danger and can destroy them and everyone around them. The identical principle is true for power, both over things and over other people.

In the hands of a mature, healthy human being—one who has achieved full humanness—power, like money or any other instrument, is a great blessing. But in the hands of the immature, vicious, or emotionally sick, power is a horrible danger.

Essentially, if you know who you are, where you are going, and what you want, then it is not hard to deal with inane bureaucratic details, trivialities, and constraints. You can simply disarm them and make them disappear by a simple shrug of your shoulders. I know that I am apt to become impatient with young people today who attribute so much power to social pressures and forces. I point out that all we need to do is pay these influences no attention, and then they vanish. Think of all the millions of dollars spent on television advertising. Such seemingly vast power becomes utterly insignificant before one who purchases products by reading consumer magazines and thereby makes intelligent judgments. The powers of evil in the American establishment suddenly disappear. For such a person, they just cease to exist.

Of course, the whole question of free will and determinism is to some extent resolved by such considerations. To use your own phrase, persons who have achieved their identity are *causers* rather than *caused*. I think it is better to frame this discussion with such words rather than *free will,* which has so many historical accretions that matters get muddled. We might say that such persons are "boss over their determinants" or that they can pick and choose their determinants, selecting those which they like and rejecting those that they dislike.

In a Spinoza-istic sense, such men and women can embrace the determinants of which they approve. Lovingly, they can let themselves be swept away by these forces akin to the manner in which a surfer rides a good wave, which is a very Taoistic activity. Certainly, the surfer does not change the wave in any way. One neither masters, controls, nor fears the wave but makes a nice, harmonious adjustment to it and, therefore, can enjoy and become a part of it.

BECOMING AUTHENTIC

I have been accustomed to say that authentic persons are those who have discovered and accepted their own, biological, temperamental, and constitutional cues, the signals from within. In a sense, this description relates to intuition as well. If you achieve this ability to hear your own impulse voices, then you have attained an inner "supreme court" from which come virtually infallible suggestions and even commands. Such people know what is good and what is bad for them and what they like and dislike.

I remember in one of your lead articles in *MANAS,*[1] you spoke about Ralph Waldo Emerson and how he trusted in his own judgments and intuitions. The verdict of history is that Emerson's judgments and intuitions were very sound and that he, therefore, was right in trusting them. But then you ended your article with a question: "How does one get to become an Emerson?"

This question could be phrased more broadly: "How does one become an identity, a sure person, one who has authentic inner voices and who hears them and has courage to act on them?" Of course, once such persons exist, then they can love themselves and do as they will.

I remember how long ago when I was teaching five psychology courses at Brooklyn College, I was so terribly busy. I was the only clinically oriented professor in the whole place, so I had to invent all sorts of tricks for providing counseling in just 2 minutes. One trick that I devised when confronted by mothers worried about their children's development was to make a quick judgment: Was the mother emotionally stable, sound, and self-respecting? If apparently so, then I counseled her as follows: "Throw away all your parenting books. Do not listen to your pediatrician. Do not ask any psychologists for advice. Just follow your own intuitions. I guarantee that they will work well on the whole, and in any case, they will work better than any advice you might receive from other people."

But if, in my judgment, the mother was emotionally unstable, neurotic, immature, or deeply confused, then I would give her a list of psychology books to read and would recommend psychotherapy for herself or her child.

Obviously, I was not being inconsistent in my method of counseling. Some people have good intuitions because they have achieved a self. Others have lousy intuitions because they have not attained a self and, therefore, cannot distinguish between the inner voices of authenticity from those of neurosis. Remember the old problem for Christians, and probably other religious believers as well, if a mystic proclaimed he or she had heard the voice of God? It could be quite reasonably asked of such people, "How can you tell whether this is the voice of God or of the devil?" This is indeed a legitimate question.

All right, then, you can say that in a certain sense, the human species is composed of perhaps 1% to 3% of people who have achieved personhood and that the vast majority have not done so and, therefore, must seek for leaders, salespersons, or priests—in a word, anyone who will tell them what to do, what to think, and so on.

EVERYONE A LEADER?

Cross-cultural evidence helps us to clarify the whole issue of leadership. It is possible for the person who is a real self, with real self-trust and self-knowledge, to know that his brother Joe is better at leading the hunting party than he is. Among the Plains Indians with whom I have studied and lived, the leader of a group was always the one who could do best at that particular task involved. They had no such thing as a general, across-the-board leader for *everything.* For this reason, the one who was a good hunter and would become the hunting party leader would quite willingly, and without resentment, subordinate himself in the war party to the one who excelled in that particular activity. Among the Blackfoot tribe, whom I knew best, leadership was determined with good will and in a *synergistic* way: Tribal members accurately knew which individual was best suited for a certain task, and there was no enmity or bitterness about assuming such responsibilities.

As the anthropologist Ruth Benedict has intimated, it seems possible—
and important—that we conceptualize, create, and invent social institutions that will either foster or hinder the development of individual self-
actualization. The operating principles or "laws" for making a good world
are different, to an extent, than for making a good person. At least to the
degree that I suggested in the beginning of this long letter to you, intrapsychic
rewards and punishments are different from external ones. We must, therefore, have a social psychology along with an individual psychology. Ultimately, both must deal meaningfully with human needs and goods.

This letter has turned out to be an article of sorts, partly because I know
we think along the same lines about the topic of leaders, pawns, and power.
I have been dictating my comments and will get them transcribed and sent
to you. It certainly would be nice if we lived closer to each other, but you
are living in Southern California and I am here in the Boston area. Even if
by machine, I enjoy talking to you. Moreover, not only do I enjoy it but I
also find it useful.

EDITOR'S NOTE

1. This was the name of the late Henry Geiger's avant-garde periodical.

Late in life, Maslow became increasingly convinced that the mass media in the United States were generally acting as a socially destructive rather than beneficial force. He strongly felt that many important, positive developments in American society were being minimized or ignored, and instead, far too much attention was being given to relatively trivial and negative events. In this unpublished, undated article written in the mid- to late 1960s, Maslow presented his viewpoint.

33

Motivational Levels of Newspapers

It may be quite useful to view newspaper content in terms of motivational theory. From the definition tacitly favored by reporters and editors as to "what is news," it seems clear that they are operating from a low, catastrophic, or safety-need-level conception. What do I mean by this? Only that which is a catastrophe, a spectacular emergency, or a horror of some sort is considered to be worthy of a newspaper headline. That is, the whole positive side of life is missing from the mainstream media.

We might say that, as a result, a tremendous "credibility gap" exists between daily reality and the typical news coverage of it. If we believe that newspapers and magazines are truly describing reality, then we simply do not know what is going on around us. For especially on television, the dominant, "catastrophic" definition of news actually *intrudes on and distorts the*

EDITOR'S NOTE: This chapter was originally printed in the Association for Humanistic Education and Development (AHEAD) newsletter. Reprinted with permission.

news—tending to reduce complex events into oversimplified, black-and-white dichotomies. Such a definition inevitably produces inaccuracies.

In most news coverage today, life is generally seen as a duel in which there are a victor and a vanquished. For instance, the president of the United States or a state governor who succeeds in pushing a bill through the legislature is reported as having won a victory over it. Or, the underlying message is that, "He got his program through!"

This outlook reminds me of the mind-set involved in jurisprudence, the courts, and of trial procedure. For the legal system too is cast in the form of a duel or a zero-sum game in which one person wins and the other loses and in which truth and justice can become lost in the process.

Another way of describing the media perspective on "news" is that it resembles the "jungle worldview" that I described long ago in my paper on the authoritarian personality (see Maslow, 1943). In this worldview, people simply are either on your side or against you, either friends or enemies. The biologist Robert Ardrey (1966) has called this outlook the "amity-enmity complex."

This lower or *Deficiency-level* conception of life should be contrasted with the higher, *Being-level* conception, which emphasizes integration, transcendence, and shades of gray rather than black-and-white dichotomies.

Besides the obvious elements of being accurate and true, what would a Being-level newspaper be like? For one thing, it would provide relatively long-lasting rather than momentary, superficial coverage. That is, it would follow up news stories instead of forgetting them the day after they occurred. As a positive example, the *Christian Science Monitor* minimizes the daily reporting of murders and other crimes or disasters like gas explosions and fires.

One could even say that such events are not really news unless there is a significant change in the rate of homicide or of deaths by accident or fire. Certainly, there is nothing new about death.

The same notion applies to many other types of commonplace newspaper stories. We hear plenty about scandals and divorces but nothing about satisfying marriages. There is much space devoted to distant battles and shooting wars like in Vietnam but virtually nothing concerning daily, ongoing life, real efforts at social improvement, or activities that might lead to beneficial future change. We have huge amounts of newspaper space devoted to juvenile delinquency but virtually none to juvenile idealism and selfless service. For instance, virtually the only time the University of California receives major newspaper coverage is when something breaks down or something bad happens there.

This dismaying situation certainly can be understood in terms of motivational theory. How? It is as though the reporters and editors of today's mainstream news media are motivated only by *Deficiency-needs* and never by *Growth-needs*. It is as if they view as newsworthy only pain and never pleasure, happiness, or joy—or only bad people and never good people.

To create a better society, this circumstance must be changed.

*ℂ As Maslow's fame grew in the field of managerial theory, he was invited
to become a scholar-in-residence (through a private grant created by
business executive William McLaughlin) at the Saga Corporation. This
was a progressive, growing institutional dining-service company based
in California. Struggling with heart disease amidst Boston's chilly clime,
Maslow eagerly accepted the attractive 4-year fellowship and, in early
1969, took an extended medical leave from Brandeis University. At Saga,
he was given a private office with full support services and invited to
speak with managers whenever the right opportunity arose. In November
1969, an ebullient Maslow offered the following remarks at the end of
observing a "retreat" held for the company's midlevel managers.*

34

The Dynamics of American Management

This has been a very good experience for me. In comparing it with similar situations, I would even say it was exceptional. Perhaps, the best service I can provide is to compare your managerial group with others. Of course, brief impressions can be unreliable. This is just one particular observational experience. But I wanted to offer my overall impressions about you as a group and then compare this organizational setup with that of others.

So first, let's talk about organizational setups. It is going to sound very corny and "square," but what I have witnessed here in the last couple of days just would not happen anywhere on the face of the earth except in the United States. That fact is well-known. This kind of advanced management is absolutely American, and it is sweeping the whole world. There is a lot of talk

184

about "American imperialism" nowadays, but the truth is that American workers simply are more efficient, desirable, and accomplished wherever they go. They just do a better job than other nationalities.

Half of this reality is due to the financial strength and vast natural resources of the United States. But the other half is due to American management, and this *managerial skill is essentially a by-product of democratic rather than aristocratic feeling.* In other places in the world, most of you would not have a chance of becoming managers at a national company like Saga, because you would not have achieved the necessary, prior promotions. There are only a few exceptions, such as Scandinavia, England, France, West Germany, and Italy, where such advancement might be possible.

I am an example of this same American dynamic. I have a high post and high status in my field. You might say that I have received many promotions and have attained the top level of my field. I am very conscious of the fact that this could not have happened in any other country in the world. My father was an immigrant. I was brought up in the slums of New York City. I am a sidewalk boy who has gone on to a marvelous vocation. I got to exactly the spot for which I was born—and that thought was running through my mind as our group talked earlier.

I do not know where you have individually come from, but the fact is that it could be anyplace. None of you needs any "pull," you do not need a well-placed relative, you do not need any hereditary privileges, you do not have to be a member of the clan, and you do not have to attend a particular school. It all depends on your own capability and talents.

I think that it might be helpful for this group—as it has been personally helpful for me—simply to become more aware of our good fortune and our plain luck in being part of this American dynamic. Why? Because individually, we do not "deserve" our heritage of freedom, vast natural resources, national political maturity, or managerial skill.

I feel grateful and privileged to be an American, and I suggest that you do too. Of course, that awareness carries with it various responsibilities and obligations.

THE OPENNESS TO EXPERIMENT

If we are indeed the lucky ones, we could regard what we are doing at the Saga Corporation as a kind of "test tube" experiment for the rest of the world.

For there is hardly any other society on earth that is affluent enough to afford to take its workers away from their workplace and sit them down just to talk with each other for a couple of days. This practice simply is not done anywhere else. And your group has made excellent use of this opportunity through your personal openness, your willingness to discuss things, and your open ear. To allocate all this time for a retreat definitely costs money, and Saga is paying a hell of a lot of money to get feedback from you as managers.

If you understand this fact, it can't help but support your self-esteem. It must make you feel good that you can affect things and that you are not a helpless pawn of fate or controlled by huge, external, impersonal forces. Each of you has an opinion about something, and so Saga is paying for the privilege of hearing you say it. For this reason, psychologists would expect you to gain in self-esteem, maturity, and emotional health.

It has been suggested that only about 5% of the general population are active agents. They are the ones who run themselves and the world. It is very clear to me that every single member of this group is one of those active agents.

You are not among the 95% who are helpless and lack direction.

Before I go into specific aspects of what I have observed, I would like to make a few general comments. First, what you have experienced the last couple of days during your retreat is true democratizing of the workplace, and it is still atypical for most organizations. As I have already mentioned, this approach of *enlightened management* hardly exists anywhere outside the United States. Even within this country, no more than 5% of companies have yet embraced the democratic ethos by really trusting their employees. So in a very real way, your group represents a great revolution in humankind's history. This principle is definitely post-Marxian. It is truly a new thing. It is as revolutionary as the ideas of Galileo, Darwin, or Freud were in their own day. It is a new way of working together.

Now with the Marxian approach to the workplace, there are inevitably adversarial conflict, struggle, and class haggles. The bosses are out to squeeze as much sweat out of the workers as possible, and the workers are out to retaliate as best as they can. That is a Marxian relationship. But we are in a different kind; we are post-Marxian because we are working together with good will and good faith. We share the assumption that it is desirable for you to do a good job—even for your own sake—in the sense that you do not think of your next level of supervisors as your innate enemies or anything like that. You have to get along with them.

This attitude shows itself in the fact that you have not behaved like a group of enemies or real rivals, in the sense of trying to "stab" or cut each other down. You have behaved like a group of colleagues, akin to U.S. senators, generals, or sovereign entities. This fact is unusual; it is definitely unusual. We can afford to be self-conscious about it. You can enjoy this self-awareness.

In short, I see your managerial retreat as a very advanced "scouting" or "pilot experiment" for all of humankind. If this workplace experiment is successful, then humankind has a very different future than that envisioned by the Marxists with their images of inevitable class warfare and strife. For my part, I feel a sense of gratitude and good fortune about all of such developments.

MANAGEMENT STYLES
(THEORY X AND THEORY Y)

I don't know how familiar you are with the recent literature on managerial and organizational styles. To put it succinctly, *Theory Y* assumes that if you give people responsibilities and freedom, then they will like to work and will do a better job. Theory Y also assumes that workers basically like excellence, efficiency, perfection, and the like.

Theory X, which still dominates most of the world's workplace, has a contrasting view. It assumes that people are basically stupid, lazy, hurtful, and untrustworthy and, therefore, that you have got to check everything constantly because workers will steal you blind if you don't.

Well, the last few days provide a marvelous example of Theory Y in action. You are all being trusted and you are all on your own, and it shows. Psychologists like myself would think that every person in this group is solid, reliable, trustworthy, and substantial. In relationship to your managerial position at Saga, you are concerned and involved, and you identify with the overall organization. It is a very lucky thing for people to enjoy their work and to identify with the entire organization, rather than to view it as pack of enemies. I can report back to you that your group showed much greater openness and courage than most. There would not be 1% of employees I have ever seen who would be able to speak so openly with one another.

EXPRESSION OF AGGRESSION

Your group displayed a certain amount of "caginess," but it was much less than I have seen elsewhere. Your relationship toward your supervisors is more open, direct, and courageous. There was not a single person who avoided the whole situation through "camouflage," as I typically would expect to see.

For example, in most situations in which I am invited to speak or observe, I have aroused considerable suspicion and defensiveness. Typically, two people are chatting to each other at the water-cooler. Then I approach, and they freeze. I have not seen that kind of anxious response here. Of course, defensiveness can emerge in all sorts of ways that psychologists can see, but essentially, you are confining it to yourselves.

The healthy means of handling aggression is to not be afraid of it. Furthermore, we must learn not to be afraid of our own aggression. It is helpful to think of it as similar to the gasoline in your automobile. Yes, it is very powerful, but it can be used productively. To deal with aggression in this manner means to be able to offer criticism: to be capable of saying, "I don't like this," or "I don't like that," or "I recommend that you do such and such" or "I recommend that you *not* do such and such."

In many places of the world, to utter such statements would result in family feuds, tribal fighting, and even death. For instance, in Japan, people do not dare to speak bluntly to one another. Everything is cloaked in politeness, indirection, and the like. Well, I would say that from my clinical viewpoint, you handled aggressive feelings very well and openly—and that sort of behavior is the mark of strong, healthy people.

OPENNESS AND DIRECTION
WITH YOUR SUPERVISOR

Your relationship with your supervisor seems to be a healthy one. Admittedly, "John" [not his real name] is a tough-minded guy and he comes on strong. If he were my boss, I think that I would be a little fearful and worried about what I would say to him. Well, I think that you handled yourselves very well—without losing your sense of dignity and autonomy in the face of a forceful character who also has power over you. This behavior I can say is unusual. It usually does not happen this way.

Generally, when there is a strong boss, everybody is involved in fawning and flattering, figuring out pleasing things to say—"kissing ass," in other words. But your supervisor asked you to talk straight to him, and you did.

Now, I am sure that you also "put your best foot forward" and engaged in a certain amount of censoring and diplomacy in your words with John. But relative to other situations, you were fairly blunt and absolutely straightforward and honest. This also means that you were strong. I would say that you were certainly among the top 5% in your ability to handle such workplace relationships.

Remember, handling aggression is a problem for many people in our society. The healthy way to do so is to become involved with people who are not afraid of one another and who know their own minds and what they want.

HANDLING OUR
FEELINGS OF AFFECTION

Especially for men in our society, another major problem is the expression of affection. We do not do this very well as a society. Others generally are more successful than ours in handling love, friendship, and physical contact. It is always possible to make judgments about how strangulated people are regarding this particular quality.

I would rate your group as above average, somewhere around the 75th percentile, in dealing with affectionate feelings. I must be honest, you are not tops! Sometimes I witnessed open displays of affection, but it was too often couched defensively—like in making jokes to cover it up. For instance, you meet your best friend and you like him. But instead of putting your arm around him, you punch him or call him an "old son of a bitch." Of course, you do not display that behavior except with your closest friends, but it is nevertheless a roundabout way of expressing affection.

Frankly, I do not know how important this issue is in your relationships. It is my view that because the workplace is structured hierarchically—that is, you have more powerful superiors and weaker subordinates—there could be warmer, more affectionate, expressive relationships in both directions. So that if you like someone or feel friendly, then you just show it. After all, organizational development groups and *t-groups* are supposed to help us develop more ability in expressing affection and friendliness.

However, your group definitely did not show *fearfulness*. You were not a strangulated group. For example, Lutheran ministers constitute perhaps the most emotionally frozen group I have observed in American society. Why this is so, I am not sure. They study texts proclaiming that "God is love," but they are unable to express any affection, or any openness, at all toward each other. Certainly, I do not get the impression that yours is a strangulated group in that sense.

Now, I have been studying the psychological characteristics of workplace executives in American society—the top executives—and this research brings up another aspect of the problem of showing affection. That is, our whole society "undersells" itself by claiming to be merely materialist. Actually, the United States is the most unmaterialist superpower that has ever existed. Yet, we keep putting on a camouflage. Our citizens—especially figures like corporate executives—are afraid of appearing corny or "square," of getting sentimental, of crying in the movies, and of looking soft.

Well, I can tell you as a psychologist that the strongest people in our society are maybe the softest—in the sense of being altruistic and idealistic. They think in terms that they would never dare to verbalize in public but that are essentially the "boy scout oath" to the highest power. Part of the American difficulty with affection, love, and sentiment is mixed up with our never-ceasing effort to look tough, strong, and invulnerable. It is as if mature adults are trying to cloak themselves in the whole adolescent interpretation of masculinity. I remember recently seeing a teenage antiwar protester on the television news. He was carrying a placard saying, "I am a man." Then, he began throwing rocks into storefront windows! Well, men do not throw rocks into windows. Only kids do.

Anyway, if I were offering recommendations to our entire society, I would advise its members to be more like Italians or Mexicans, who are a little more openly expressive of affection.

MANLINESS

The definition of adult masculinity—of what a fully grown, mature man is like—certainly includes softness, that is, the ability to become sentimental and affectionate. It is only the adolescent male who does not dare to show his affection. You know, adolescents today find it very hard to display affection because that behavior appears weak. So unfortunately, they miss out on many good things.

Well, your group expressed plenty of positive remarks here. When someone had something good to express, it was clearly stated. That is a mature, psychologically healthy attitude. It is typical of the man who feels authentically self-confident and who can, therefore, be tender. But if you lack self-confidence, then you have to act tough all the time and consequently to overdo tough behavior.

OUR INNER PICTURE OF PEOPLE

One thing that I can recommend for you, especially if you are seeking promotions and greater responsibilities, is that your judgments about people could be improved by becoming more varied, that is, deeper and fuller. Unfortunately, your statements in this regard were rather skimpy.

For instance, your group had a role-playing exercise in which you were invited to make statements about one another. Well, from a psychological perspective, your comments generally were shallow. People are so complicated, so rich, and so varied! My impression is that you feel restrained in expressing interpersonal relationships or making interpersonal judgments. If I can make a recommendation here, it is that you can be more successful simply by looking more carefully and persistently at people. Try to make a richer, more complex picture than the one you have made. Of course, any brief picture—for example, "Describe someone you know by using only two words"—may be wrong. That is where feedback comes in.

Now, I do not know whether your shortcoming in this respect relates more to a problem in expression or in your inner portraits of one another. My hunch is that it is the former.

As managers, you have to deal with people all the time. If you did not do this task well, then you would quickly be out of a job. So, my guess is that you are intuitive, perceptive, and diplomatic in interpersonal relationships far more than you are able to articulate or discuss. But it is very desirable to be able to talk these feelings out because you must write down your estimates and judgments of people. Because talking about your perceptions also causes them to become more *conscious* rather than *unconscious,* I would advise you to initiate more discussions.

SIMILARITIES AND DIFFERENCES

The similarities among each of you are greater than the differences. I will say it again: By comparison with others, your group is composed of people who are very much alike in the characteristics that I have mentioned. That is, each one of you gives me the impression of strength, solidity, reliability, and dependability. My conjecture is that you do your job well. For instance, I have gotten the definite feeling that I could really rely on each of you— without exception—in an emergency.

Of course, individual differences exist among you. But as far as your work is concerned, what I have just said indeed applies. My impression is that you each have all the necessary qualities for placing at the top 5th percentile of leadership in this society or any other society. It is this top 5%, you know, who get necessary things done and who keep a society going effectively. It is this same 5% who are the most responsible and who, in effect, lead and support the other 95% of citizens. So far as your work at Saga is concerned, your individual differences are less significant.

OUR PROFESSIONALISM

For what it is worth—because it is just my impression—I think you would benefit from reading more about the intellectual backdrop to your job. As I have been saying today, "You are leaders not only for America, but for the entire world." We are sort of the pilots for other nations because they lack the money, the time, and the efficiency to accomplish what we have learned about management right here in this retreat. So, I recommend that you do more reading in the rich literature of managerial theory.

If I had one book to suggest, it would be Douglas McGregor's (1960) *The Human Side of Enterprise.* It usually serves as the introduction to a whole line of thinking. A more recent, excellent book by McGregor (1967) is *The Professional Manager.* Such volumes would help to provide a conceptual framework—a wider context—for your daily work at Saga, with all its de-tails. By reading such books, you would not only become effective managers but also improve your promotability. So there is another example of *synergy* at work!

Here we have the merging of self-interest and altruism, of self-interest and other-interest. In the best situations, this synergy always occurs. For instance, if you get along well with your spouse in a marriage, you eventually realize that narrow self-interest ceases to exist. You are one person, but you are inevitably also part of a team. There is a pooling of interests.

Well, in the field of enlightened management—enlightened industry—this same merging of interests takes place. If you do a good job at Saga, then you are benefiting yourself, the company, the country, and ultimately the entire world. If America could fulfill the American dream a little more fully, we could help fulfill a world dream.

Our country has sometimes been criticized badly in the international press, but the American dream still beckons. You know, if the doors to our country were completely opened, then probably 98% of humankind would want to enter. That is a kind of voting with one's feet! So the American dream still beckons.

If you do your own job better, and I think you all can, and if you are more Olympian—gazing down as though from a great height at your daily routine—then you gain a better perspective of how everything fits together. By reading stimulating books, you can attain some of that wider outlook.

Of course, reading generally will help you to get along better with other people. That is good for you personally and for the entire world. So I really recommend that you read more.

CONCLUSION

Thanks for allowing me to observe your managerial retreat. Your willingness to do so is itself a sign of maturity, for many groups would have refused my attendance. Its members would have become tense and ill at ease in the presence of a psychologist. People tend to run away from psychologists due to deluded fears about our X-ray eyes or our ability to "read minds."

In this context, I would like to end with a humorous anecdote. I was recently attending a big party when a young woman walked into the room. She was stunning physically, and I found myself staring at her beauty. I was momentarily overwhelmed by her physical attractiveness. Suddenly, the young woman noticed me staring at her and strode right over. Stepping close, she said, "I know what you're thinking!"

Taken aback, I awkwardly managed to stammer, "You do?" "Yes," she smiled triumphantly. "I know that you're a psychologist, and so you're trying to psychoanalyze me!"

And I laughed and replied, "Well, that's *not* what I was thinking of!"

So, I take your willingness to allow my presence here during retreat to be a sign of self-confidence, lack of fear, and emotional healthfulness. To accept me, as a psychologist, in your midst is significant, and I personally appreciate it. For me, it has been a very interesting and inspiring couple of days.

Throughout Maslow's life, he argued strongly that psychology—and science in general—needed to be more open to new ideas and paradigms. Though never conducting research on extrasensory perception (ESP), Maslow believed that sufficient evidence existed for it to be viewed as a subject worthy of serious scientific investigation. In this letter dated May 17, 1966, he shared his viewpoint with Dr. J. B. Rhine, who pioneered parapsychology in the United States.

Letter to J. B. Rhine

Dr. J. B. Rhine
Institute for Parapsychology
College Station
Durham, North Carolina

Dear Dr. Rhine:

It was so pleasant meeting you, even briefly, that I forgot to discuss with you a thought that I've had at various times.

It has seemed to me that in the study of loving couples, or of intimate love relationships of any other kind, that somehow there are many coincidences, unspoken communications, anticipations of wishes, and the like. Certainly, the nonverbal communications by loving people are more efficient than by others. If I were to do any research on ESP, it seems to me that this is the kind of subject that I would prefer to use.

195

My question is: Has anybody ever worked on this, are there any systematic data—anything that could be called research? (I assume, of course, that there must be many anecdotes.)

Cordially,
A. H. Maslow

@ Ironically enough, Maslow's humanistic approach often has been described as anti-behaviorist. Yet, Maslow himself began his psychological career as an ardent experimentalist trained in behaviorism. Though certainly moving well beyond that orientation, Maslow always bore respect for the behaviorist position as one of several important and necessary facets of modern psychology. He objected only to those who would make behaviorism, or experimentalism, the only means toward psychological knowledge. As this letter dated April 5, 1965, to B. F. Skinner reveals, Maslow was on cordial terms with America's leading behaviorist thinker for many decades.

Letter to B. F. Skinner

Dr. B. F. Skinner
Department of Psychology
Harvard University
Cambridge, MA 02138

Dear Fred:

Thank you for your letter *and* for its bluntness, which is helpful.

If values and the life of values are your professional concern, poetry, art, and so on, you must make a better theoretical place in your structure for experiential knowledge. At least, it must be accepted as a beginning of knowledge and this must be done in a *systematic* way (as part of the theory of science). I think this is quite compatible with my methodological or epistemological behaviorism that thinks of objective, public, respectable knowledge as most reliable, most certain, most solid, an ideal toward which to press. But there is no need to exclude experience as datum for science and then to hope to objectify it eventually.

Beyond that, what you choose to specialize in is a matter of (characterological) taste. I like playing around with the beginnings of knowledge, raising new questions, and so on. Other people like to work on more solid ground. Both approaches are okay. I think I know both pleasures. It was John B. Watson's writings that brought me into psychology. At the University of Wisconsin, Clark Hull, Norman Cameron, Bill Sheldon, and everyone else was a behaviorist—and so was I. All my research was in this line. The feeling of building something solid, firm, and reliable is a very good one. But it need not exclude the speculating, groping, trying things out in some preliminary, heuristic way.

For instance, my analysis of *Being-values* is very meaningful to me, and it keeps on groping to express matters in ways that are thus far poetic and figurative. Well, I am very confident that I am pointing in the direction of a dimly cognizable reality, which one day we will know well enough to put to the test, objectify, confirm, or disconfirm. Let's check on this in 10 years.

I am so interested in what you say of your *peak-experiences* and of your interest in the impulsive, emotional, and so on. May I suggest that you expand on this in your autobiography? It will correct the erroneous picture people have. I accept the correction and am glad to hear about it. Also, about translating your stuff [into behavioral language] as you were reading it. It is good that it is translatable.

Yes, please send me your writings on these matters when you finish them.

Cordially,
A. H. Maslow

During Maslow's last years, he became quite interested in applying his system of humanistic psychology to the crucial domain of public policy. He felt convinced that such psychological knowledge—including such concepts as the hierarchy of inborn needs, higher motivation, and self-actualization—could play a powerful role in creating a more harmonious American society and larger world order. Written on May 8, 1970, a month before Maslow's death, this unpublished letter summarizes well his perspective on public policy.

Letter to John D. Rockefeller III

Mr. John D. Rockefeller III
Room 5600
30 Rockefeller Plaza
New York, New York 10020

Dear Mr. Rockefeller:

I found your Manila talk on "The Quality of Life" interesting, and even fascinating, for reasons beyond the overt face value of the common sense and good judgment of the paper itself. In addition to this, I was extremely absorbed by the convergence between the results of your personal thinking and probing and final judgments on one hand, and the very similar conclusions that come from the findings of the psychotherapists, the theoretical psychologists, the management scientists, and so on. They too have found that part of the human essence is what you have called human dignity,

199

belonging, attaining full potential, caring, and beauty. I have gone so far as to coin a word for these basic needs and aspirations of human nature. I call them *instinctoid,* to indicate by belief that the evidence makes them defining qualities of human nature itself, aspects of its essence, aspects of specieshood.

I am sure also that you will find of the greatest interest my finding that self-actualizing people, that is, people who have been reasonably gratified in their needs for safety, belongingness, affection, dignity, and freedom to develop their own personal potentialities, that such people then become motivated no longer by their *basic needs* but, rather, by what I have called *metamotives*—but which turn out to be essentially the intrinsic values, the eternal verities, the values of Being. These include, as you have pointed out, beauty. But also there is considerable evidence to show that you can add to fill out the picture of these *metaneeds* truth, excellence, order (in the mathematical sense), unity, perfection, and so on.

For me this has been a very heartening thing, to realize that at least for some human beings—I don't know what percentage yet—as the basic aspects that make up the quality of life become fulfilled, they can move on to higher and higher aspirations. That is to say that if there was fulfillment of the aspects of the quality of life that you have listed, you could confidently expect that at least some human beings would move on to become more fully human, closer to the ideally good person. This is not to say that they would be saints, because I also have found that aspirations never cease (or to say it in a negative way, that grumbling, complaining, and wanting more and more never cease). One can say this in an encouraging way—that man's aspirations are endless and higher and higher—or one can say it in a negative way. In any case, we have evidence to indicate that the static notion of the good person, or of the good society, or even of the good heaven, must all give way to the person or the society reaching ever higher and higher and higher, to levels that we cannot even conceive of today.

Let me add my personal gratitude that you used your influence to focus simultaneously on that which is immediately urgent and sine qua non, in this case population control, but also found it possible to talk about aspirations that go beyond our most immediate and urgent problems. As I mentioned in our conversation, I find it extremely helpful, even in the middle of today's turmoil, in the middle of the hurricane so to speak, to have in my hand a compass that tells me the direction toward which I must steer even through the storm and beyond it. I know that it is easy to fall into the utopian spirit and think only of far-off ideals, and I agree with you that this is a great danger.

Yet it is equally dangerous, I feel, to focus oneself entirely and exclusively on the immediate, on the fire that is raging now, without also thinking about tomorrow, next year, the next generation, and even the next century. Having this kind of compass helps me, at least, to know what to do at this moment, today, in the middle of an immediately demanding problem.

Of the various basic needs that have been discovered, you have covered them all but one, which I would certainly recommend that you add. This is the need for safety, security, stability, continuity, trust in the environment. I would use the words law and order here if they have not developed particular political accretions of meaning. But those would be fair words to use as aspects of the basic needs for safety, security, and so on. This is an especial problem in the underdeveloped countries (for instance, in Mexico, which I studied for a time): the law itself cannot be trusted, policemen and public officials must be bribed and they are not public servants but care for their own selfish interests first. Or it could be said in another way: where there is violence on the campuses and in the streets; where fear reigns after dark; where the government, the army, the police all seem helpless to ensure the ability to walk without anxiety, without fear, let us say, through Central Park. This is a profound and basic and instinctoid need of all human beings as a species. It is perfectly true that this can be subsumed under the material needs, or even of belongingness, but I have found it helpful to separate it out and to speak of it as a separable need that commands attention and ful-fillment.

Another general scientific finding that I think would be helpful to you in your thinking about the quality of life is the finding that these basic needs are organized into what I have called a "hierarchy of prepotency." That is, although these are all universal human needs that demand gratification on pain of developing illness, some of them are more urgent, more prepotent, more demanding than others. The hierarchy of prepotency is an order of urgency or demandingness. The findings are so far that most urgent are the material needs; then come the safety-security needs; then comes belong-ingness; then come loving and caring, friendship, and affection; then come respect and self-respect and dignity; and then, finally, comes fulfilling one's own individual potentials, what I have called self-actualization. As you point out, self-actualization or dignity and so on are quite expendable when the person is hungry.

Certain basic needs are more urgent than others. This same hierarchy, or something very much like it, has been found to exist, for instance, not only in the order of priority of unconscious needs in the neurotic person but also in the history of what labor unions have struck for, the order of urgency of the problems of the underdeveloped nations, the order of kinds of satisfactions and kinds of pay that upwardly mobile and economically successful individuals in the United States seek for, the order of importance of the human needs that supervisors and managers had better satisfy in our factories, and so on. That is to say, it looks like a universal individual and social principle.

I do hope that these remarks may be helpful. Perhaps they will help you to see why I so much enjoyed your paper.

Cordially,
A. H. Maslow

Glossary of Maslow's Terms

Abraham Maslow coined many terms in developing his influential psychological thought. Over the decades, some of these terms have come to circulate throughout the wider world of social science and even Western culture as a whole. Nevertheless, some of Maslow's most important terms have been consistently misunderstood and misapplied. At the time of his death, he had begun to voice dismay over the increasingly distorted representations of his ideas. The following key terms are defined briefly here as he used them in his writings.

Aggridant A biologically superior member of a species, human or otherwise; a better perceiver and chooser. Tends to occupy a dominant or leadership position in the social order of that species. Also known as *alpha*.

Alpha See *aggridant*. Derived from Aldous Huxley's usage in his novel *Brave New World*.

Apollonian mystic One who experiences transcendence and the sacred through contemplation.

Basic needs Inborn, *instinctoid*, lower psychological needs. In hierarchical order, from bottom to top, they are the needs for safety and protection, belongingness, love, respect, and self-esteem. Also known as *Deficiency-needs* or *lower needs*.

Being-art (B-art) Art that expresses one or more of the *B-values*.

Being-cognition (B-cognition) Clear, contemplative knowing, especially of transcendent, sacred, and eternal aspects of a person or thing. Occurs most often in *self-actualizing* people, though not exclusively, during a *peak-experience*.

203

Being-guilt   Appropriate, healthy guilt, which results from a betrayal of our higher nature or the *B-values,* like justice or truth, in our lives. Also called *intrinsic guilt.*

Being-humor (B-humor)   Philosophical or enlightening humor, reflecting a high level of maturity and motivation, for example, the quality of humor associated with Abraham Lincoln. Also known as *self-actualizing humor* or *existential humor.*

Being-knowledge (B-knowledge)   Knowledge of the transcendent, unique, or sacred inherent in a person or thing, gained through *B-cognition* rather than through logic or rationality.

Being-language (B-language)   Words that seek to express *B-values,* such as through an experience involving ecstasy or bliss.

Being-love (B-love)   Unselfish, unconditioned regard for the nature and potentialities of the loved one, rather than use of the loved one to gratify one's own *basic needs;* loving something precisely the way it is, in its uniqueness.

Being-motivation (B-motivation)   See *metamotivation.*

Being-needs (B-needs)   Also known as *growth needs* or *metaneeds.*

Being-realm   See *Being-world.*

Being-values (B-values)   The intrinsic and ultimate human values, such as truth, beauty, and justice. They are the objects of our *metaneeds* and the goal of our *metamotivations.*

Being-world (B-world)   The higher, experiential realm involving the *B-values.*

Bodhisattva   Buddhist term for one who, having attained personal enlightenment, selflessly returns to the everyday world to serve as a teacher and helper for others.

Countervalues   Fear, hatred, or resentment expressed toward the *B-values* or toward virtue in general.

Countervaluing   Experiencing or expressing hostility toward the *B-values* or what embodies them, such as debunking or devaluing. This is a psychological defense against feeling awe or wonder in the presence of the *B-values,* due to the resentment they can arouse in us because of our deficiencies.

Deficiency-cognition (D-cognition)   Ordinary knowing, such as through logic or rational analysis, in which people or things are seen in their isolated details.

Deficiency-humor (D-humor)   Hostile, cruel, or belittling humor, such as laughing at another's misfortune; reflects a low level of maturity or motivation.

Deficiency-love (D-love)   Regard for the loved one's capacity to satisfy our own *basic needs.*

Deficiency-motivation (D-motivation)   Motivation related to satisfy our *basic needs.*

Deficiency-needs (D-needs)   See *basic needs.*

Deficiency-realm   See *Deficiency-world.*

Deficiency-values (D-values)   Values that relate to *Deficiency-motivation* and *Deficiency-needs.*

Deficiency-world (D-world)   The experiential realm in which the *Deficiency-values* predominate.

Dionysian mystic   One who experiences transcendence and the sacred through wild exuberance.

Enlightened management   Incorporates the principles of humanistic psychology, especially the fostering of personality growth and creativity of organizational members, products and services, and the overall well-being of the organization. Also known as *eupsychian management.*

Eupsychia   By formal definition, the culture that would be generated by 1,000 *self-actualized* people on an isolated island; more broadly, the most perfect society that human nature can permit, which satisfies the *basic needs* and presents the possibility for *self-actualization* of all its members.

Eupsychian   Moving toward *eupsychia*—that is, toward achievable psychological health; connotes real improvement rather than mere utopian traits. Also, the actions taken to foster and encourage such a movement by a teacher, therapist, or manager; refers to the mental, social, or organizational conditions that make health more likely.

Growth-needs   See *metaneeds.*

Hierarchy of needs   The inborn array of physiological and psychological needs encompassing the *basic needs* and *metaneeds.* As a lower need is fulfilled within us, a new and higher need tends to emerge.

Homeostatic politics   Political activity designed to advance society toward *eupsychia* while sustaining stability and order.

Humanistic psychology   Popularized in the 1960s, the term refers to the broad-based psychology that Maslow, Rollo May, Carl Rogers, and others helped to establish, which seeks to transcend the schools of psychoanalysis and behaviorism. Also known as the *Third Force.*

Instinctoid needs   Inborn psychological needs, encompassing *basic needs* and *metaneeds.* Although weak in nature, these cause us to desire and seek out certain values, such as beauty or truth, in our lives. The gratification of instinctoid needs is necessary for complete health.

Intrinsic guilt   See *Being-guilt.*

Intrinsic self   The authentic self.

Intrinsic values   Those human values that are *instinctoid* and that we need to satisfy in order to avoid illness and achieve full growth; deprivation of the intrinsic values leads to *metapathologies*. Also, the object of the *metaneeds*.

Jonah complex   Based on the biblical figure of Jonah, this emotional condition reflects a "fear of one's own greatness" and results in a fear of doing what we do best and evasion of our own potentialities. In daily life, the Jonah complex can take the form of a low level of aspiration.

Lower needs   See *basic needs*.

Metacounselor   A counselor who advises people on how to experience the *B-values* through a vocation or other means.

Metagratification   The sense of gratification through experiencing one or more of the *B-values*.

Metamotivation   Motivational state of yearning for the *B-values*, like truth, beauty, justice, perfection; the dominant motivation in a self-actualizing person.

Metaneeds   Inborn though weak psychological needs that lie beyond the *basic needs;* these are our needs for the *B-values*. Their deprivation leads to *meta-pathologies* or "sicknesses of the soul."

Metapathologies   The spiritual-existential ailments that result from the persistent deprivation of *metaneeds*—the lack of fulfillment of *metamotivations*. They include cynicism, apathy, boredom, loss of zest, despair, hopelessness, a sense of powerlessness, and nihilism.

Peak-experience   An ordinarily brief and transient moment of bliss, rapture, ecstasy, great happiness, or joy. We usually feel such emotions as awe, reverence, and wonder in such moments; also, we feel more alive, integrated, "here and now," and yet in touch with the transcendent and the sacred; more frequent in self-actualizing people.

Plateau-experience   A serene and calm, rather than intensely emotional, response to what we experience as miraculous or awesome. The high plateau always has a noetic and cognitive element, unlike the *peak-experience,* which can be merely emotional; it is also far more volitional than the peak-experience.

Psychopolitics   Political theory or action derived from the principles of humanistic psychology, especially the *hierarchy of needs*.

Safety needs   Inborn psychological needs for feeling a sense of physical security; a type of *basic need*.

Self   The biologically based core of the personality.

Self-actualization   The apex of personal growth, in which we become freed from *basic needs* and *deficiency motivation;* not an endpoint in most people but a drive or yearning to fully develop. Also, the process of fulfilling our latent talents, capacities, and potentialities at any time, in any amount. Although we all have this drive, we also possess a fear of growth.

Self-actualized person   A psychologically healthy, mature, and self-fulfilled individual, whose *basic needs* are met and who is, therefore, motivated by *metaneeds* and an active seeking of the *B-values.* Such a person tends to have certain specific traits, including creativity, sagacity, emotional spontaneity, and commitment to a calling. Also known as *self-actualizer.*

Self-actualizing humor   See *Being-humor.*

Synergic   Having the quality of *synergy;* also, the extent to which individuals and organizational/societal needs or goals are mutually enhanced. For example, a synergic society "is one in which virtue pays."

Synergy   Term coined by anthropologist Ruth Benedict in 1941, then elaborated and popularized by Maslow. A high-synergy culture is one in which what is beneficial for the individual is simultaneously beneficial for everyone, and vice versa; for example, a culture that generously rewards altruistic behavior. A low-synergy culture is one in which what is good for the individual is harmful for others, and vice versa; for example, an organization in which one's success can occur only at the expense of others.

Taoist   Having the quality of receptivity and surrender; being nonintrusive and noninterfering.

Taoist helper   A counselor, therapist, or other individual with Taoist qualities.

T-group (Training-group)   Developed by humanistic counselors like Carl Rogers, these were created to facilitate direct, honest, and helpful communication among individuals, such as in organizational settings.

Theory Z   Managerial theory formulated by Maslow that seeks to synthesize and transcend the influential Theory X and Theory Y dichotomy advanced by Douglas McGregor in 1960.

Third force   See *humanistic psychology.*

Value pathology   See *metapathology.*

References

Adorno, T. W., Frenkel-Brunswick, E., Levinson, D. J., & Sanford, R. N. (1950). *The authoritarian personality.* New York: Harper & Row.

Angyal, A. (1965). *Neurosis and treatment: A holistic theory.* New York: John Wiley.

Ardrey, R. (1966). *The territorial imperative.* New York: Atheneum.

Asch, S. (1965). *Social psychology.* Englewood Cliffs, NJ: Prentice Hall.

Bodkin, M. (1934). *Archetypal patterns in poetry.* London: Oxford University Press.

Bugental, J. (1965). *The search for authenticity.* New York: Holt, Rinehart & Winston.

Fergusson, H. (1971). *The blood of the conquerors.* New York: Arno. (Original work published 1921)

Fiedler, L. (1968). Greek mythologies. *Encounter, 30*(4), 41-55.

Frankl, V. (1984). *Man's search for meaning* (3rd ed.). New York: Simon & Schuster.

Freud, A. (1950). *The ego and the mechanisms of defense* (C. Baines, Trans.). New York: International Universities Press.

Friedan, B. (1963). *The feminine mystique.* New York: Norton.

Fromm, E. (1939). Selfishness and self-love. *Psychiatry, 2,* 507-523.

Hoffman, E. (1988). *The right to be human: A biography of Abraham Maslow.* Los Angeles: Tarcher.

Huxley, A. (1964). *The perennial philosophy.* New York: Harper.

James, W. (1981). *The principles of psychology.* Cambridge, MA: Harvard University Press. (originally ublished in 1890)

Koestler, A. (1960). *The lotus and the robot.* London: Hutchinson.

Krishnamurti, J. (1954). *The first and last freedom.* New York: Harper.

Lewis, C. S. (1956). *Surprised by joy.* New York: Harcourt Brace.

Manuel, F. (1968). *A portrait of Isaac Newton.* Cambridge, MA: Harvard University Press.

Maslow, A. H. (1937). Personality and patterns of culture. In R. Stagner (Ed.), *Psychology of personality* (pp. 89-111). New York: McGraw-Hill.

Maslow, A. H. (1943). The authoritarian character structure. *Journal of Social Psychology, 18,* 401-411.

Maslow, A. H. (1954). *Motivation and personality.* New York: Harper & Brothers.

Maslow, A. H. (1959). Cognition of being in the peak experiences. *Journal of Genetic Psychology, 94*, 43-66.

Maslow, A. H. (1964). *Religions, values, and peak-experiences*. Columbus: Ohio University Press.

Maslow, A. H. (1965). *Eupsychian management: A journal*. Homewood, IL: Irwin-Dorsey.

Maslow, A. H. (1967). A theory of meta-motivation: The biological rooting of the value-life. *Journal of Humanistic Psychology, 7*, 93-127.

Maslow, A. H. (1968a). Music education and peak-experiences. *Music Educator's Journal, 54*, 72-75, 163-171.

Maslow, A. H. (1968b). *Toward a psychology of being* (2nd ed.). Princeton: Van Nostrand. (Original work published 1962)

Maslow, A. H. (1971). *The farther reaches of human nature*. New York: Viking.

Maslow, A. H., & Mittelman, B. (1941). *Principles of abnormal psychology*. New York: Harper & Brothers.

Matson, F. (1966). *The broken image*. Garden City, NY: Doubleday.

McClelland, D. C. (1953). *The achievement motive*. Norwalk, CT: Appleton-Century-Crofts.

McClelland, D. C. (1961). *The achieving society*. Princeton, NJ: Van Nostrand.

McGregor, D. (1960). *The human side of enterprise*. New York: McGraw-Hill.

McGregor, D. (1967). *The professional manager* (W. G. Bennis & C. McGergor, Eds.). New York: McGraw-Hill.

Northrop, F. S. (1979). *The meeting of east and west*. New York: Macmillan. (Original work published 1946)

Polyani, M. (1964). *Science, faith, and society*. Chicago: University of Chicago Press.

Rogers, C. (1940). *Counseling and psychotherapy*. Boston: Houghton Mifflin.

Shostrom, E. (1963). *Personal orientation inventory (POI): A test of self-actualization*. San Diego, CA: Educational and Industrial Testing Service.

Skinner, B. F. (1962). *Walden two*. New York: Macmillan.

Sohl, J. (1967). *The lemon eaters*. New York: Simon & Schuster.

Solzhenitsyn, A. (1969). *Cancer ward*. New York: Farrar, Straus & Giroux.

Sorokin, P. (1954). *Forms and techniques of altruistic and spiritual growth*. Boston: Beacon.

Stagner, R. (Ed.). (1937). *Psychology of personality*. New York: McGraw-Hill.

Sumner, W. G. (1940). *Folkways*. New York: Ginn and Company.

Wilson, C. (1959). *The stature of man*. Boston: Houghton Mifflin.

Wilson, C. (1964). *The outsider*. London: Arthur Baker.

Yablonsky, L. (1968). *Hippie trip*. New York: Penguin.

Zaleznik, A. (1956). *Worker satisfaction and development*. Boston: Harvard University Graduate School of Business Administration.

Zaleznik, A. (1966). *Human dilemmas of leadership*. New York: Harper & Row.

Index

About the Editor

Edward Hoffman is a licensed clinical psychologist in the New York City area. He received his doctorate from the University of Michigan and is the author of more than 75 articles and several books in psychology and related fields. These include *The Drive for Self: Alfred Adler and the Founding of Individual Psychology, Visions of Innocence: Spiritual and Inspirational Experiences of Childhood,* and *The Right to Be Human: A Biography of Abraham Maslow.* He lectures frequently around the United States on humanistic and spiritual aspects of psychotherapy. His writings have been translated into Danish, French, German, and Japanese. He lives on Long Island with his wife and two children.